THE PULP JUNGLE

The Pulp Jungle

by Frank Gruber

SHERBOURNE PRESS, INC.
Los Angeles, California

Copyright © 1967 by Frank Gruber

Library of Congress Catalog Card Number: 67–21873

Manufactured in the United States of America.

First printing

Chapter One

Late in 1960 I received a telephone call from a professor at the University of California at Los Angeles. They were having a special exhibit of *Black Mask* magazines and material about *Black Mask* writers, and the professor wondered if I was the Frank Gruber who had contributed to the magazine back in the 1930's.

To say that I was startled is the understatement of the week. Me, a relic of the dinosauric period of pulp writing?

On exhibit?

But the calendar is a brutal thing, and in 1960 it was twenty years since I had written my last story for *Black Mask*. It is now twenty-seven years and I have become somewhat attuned to the fact that I am an old mossback who has somehow survived his time and in these past six or seven years I have seen many, many stories reprinted from the *Black Mask* period, and I have seen and heard many critics and students of serious literature extol the virtues and vitality of those practitioners of the sparse prose of the 1930's.

A writer is seldom a modest person—if he were he would not be a writer—and since I lived and practiced my craft through those years I hope that the reader will bear with me through the continual use of the "I" that I cannot avoid in reminiscing about the life and times of the pulp writers of the 1930's.

*　　*　　*

There are milestones along the path of anyone's life and there were times in my own career when memorable things happened—memorable to me, that is, but being a writer I cannot merely put a character on a road and have him set down milestones here and there. I've got to give the character some substance. I've got to give him a background. I've got to probe his mind. I've got to give him some depth and I've got to tell how he came to be on that road. *I've got to make him come alive.*

So there is only one place to start—at the beginning.

*　　*　　*

I read my first book when I was nine years old. It was a paperback copy of *Luke Walton, The Chicago Newsboy* by Horatio Alger, Jr. The book made a profound impression upon me, for I lived in Chicago and I was, at the age of nine, a newsboy!

During the next several years I read a hundred Alger books. Some I borrowed, some I stole, some I got from the Chicago Public Library, a few were given to me as birthday or Christmas gifts and some I bought myself, in the Donahue cloth editions, which sold in those days for ten cents.

The Alger books influenced me more than anything

else in my life. They settled the problem of my future. They instilled in me an ambition that I have had from the age of nine or ten. I never deviated from that early ambition.

Virtually all of the Horatio Alger, Jr., books have the same theme—they tell how poor boys became rich. The theme inspired three generations of Americans. Alas! The reading of the Alger books did not instill in me the ambition to become a rich businessman. No, the books inspired me to become a writer, to write books like those of Horatio Alger, Jr. And I was writing before I was eleven. I completed at that time a book. It was written in pencil on wrapping paper, cut down to appropriate size.

Of course I outgrew the Alger books, but I did not outgrow the desire to become a writer. But life had to be lived in the meantime and I quit scribbling when I was about thirteen or fourteen.

The flame of ambition smoldered during the years and sometimes it became a dim flicker, but it never died out entirely, and in my late teens and early twenties the flame became sturdy. But by that time I had become a young intellectual and when I began writing again I was reading *Literature* with a capital L.

I wrote stories and submitted them to magazines like the old *Smart Set*, *Atlantic Monthly* and *Scribner's Magazine*. They were all rejected and I thought I would lower my sights and try the more popular magazines, *The Saturday Evening Post*, *Collier's*, that type of trash. They wanted none of me and I found myself, at the age of twenty-two, with the ambition to write burning more brightly than ever, but nowhere to go.

The pulp magazines had begun to flower and I started reading them. I wrote a few stories and mailed them to the pulps. I was still living in Chicago, but I had, at this point, never met a real live editor and I would not have known an author if I had seen one on the street!

A few magazines were still published in Chicago in those days and one day I decided to go down in person and meet an editor. The magazine was *Real Detective* and the editor, one Edwin Baird, made a big thing in the back of the magazine about his writers. He was always "discovering" new writers and he welcomed them to his magazine.

I took a day off from my regular job and went down to see Mr. Baird. I got into his office, all right, but he kept me standing and gave me about thirty seconds of his valuable time. I handed him a manuscript. I will say this, he sent it back with a personal note—instead of the familiar rejection slip. The substance of the note was "forget it."

I wasn't willing to forget it, and one Saturday I went downtown to McClurg's Book Store and came across a book entitled, *1001 Places to Sell Manuscripts*. I also found a magazine called *Writer's Digest*.

These two items opened up a new world. I found that there were hundreds and hundreds of publications that were not usually found on the newsstands that printed stories and paid for them.

Weeks of study of the magazine and the book decided me to try the lowest form of writing—at least that was the way it seemed to me at the time. There were about a hundred Sunday School papers that paid from a tenth of a cent a word to a half cent. There was a hint in *1001 Places to Sell Manuscripts* that sample copies of these papers could be obtained free. I bought a hundred postcards and brazenly wrote to every paper listed, asking for a free copy.

Astonishingly, almost all of the Sunday School publishing houses sent me free copies of their publications! I read them thoroughly and for six months wrote Sunday School stories and mailed them to the little church papers. The stories came back with monotonous regularity. Each was accompanied by a printed rejection slip.

It was an agonizing period. I was twenty-three years of age. I had read Jack London's *Martin Eden* and thinking about it was about the only thing that kept me going. London had had just as difficult a time breaking in. But he hadn't stooped to writing the lowly Sunday School stories and if I couldn't sell even *those*, what hope was there for me?

I continued to send out the stories. I even retyped some that had become shabby from much traveling in the United States mails. I mailed them, took them out of the return envelopes and mailed them again. It became a routine thing.

And then one day I opened an envelope. It was rather thin but I had thin stories out as well as fat ones. This envelope didn't contain a rejection slip, however. It had a letter—and a check for three dollars and fifty cents. The United Brethren Publishing House of Dayton, Ohio, was accepting my story, "The Two Dollar Raise."

I had made it.

Chapter Two

I was an author.

The time was February, 1927.

That same week I answered an advertisement in the *Chicago Tribune* and—on the strength of being a *published* author—got a job as editor of a small farm paper. I kept the job until September when I got a higher-paying editorial post in Iowa, to which I traveled and where I lived for the next four years.

I became editor, eventually, of five farm papers and was even a stockholder in the company. A problem soon arose. I was so successful in the farm paper field and my salary became so large that I could not afford to take time off to write stories for outside publications. I wrote many articles for the farm papers, however, as part of my job, and once in a great while I wrote a story. By early 1932 I had published a grand total of seven stories in various Sunday School publications and had even had a poem published in one of the little poetry magazines that did not pay for contributions.

My writing problem was solved in 1932, however. The

Depression was on but I had weathered it rather well. Now came the Big Crash. The company I had been with for almost five years became involved in a merger. The merged company went into bankruptcy and I was out of a job. I had been married the year before and I scrambled around seeking a job. There were none—not in 1932.

I made the Big Decision. Since there were no jobs to be had, I would become a writer.

We went to Webster Groves, Missouri (a suburb of St. Louis), and moved in with my wife's family. We had a room and received our meals, but it was up to me to earn any money we would have to spend.

Three years ago, while searching my old files for a letter once written to me by a literary agent, telling me how bad I was, I found at the back of a file an old ledger which I had not seen in over twenty years. I did not even recall having kept such a ledger, but there it was in front of me.

The ledger contained a complete record of my writing life from August, 1932, through June, 1934. The record is a thorough one, containing names, dates and amounts.

Shortly after finding this ledger I was booked to address a ladies' literary club and I decided to use the figures as part of my talk. A writer who followed me on the program said that it was the most gruesome horror story he had ever heard in his life.

I will recount it here.

The journal covers the period from August, 1932,

through June, 1934, when I went to New York, but the really desperate period lasted only from August, 1932, until April 1, 1933, when I got a job. But I continued to write evenings while on this job and these writings are in the record.

From August, 1932, through June, 1934, I wrote a grand total of one hundred seventy-four "pieces." The total wordage amounted to six hundred twenty thousand words, the equivalent of about eight books.

I have tried, through the years, to forget this period, but you cannot forget everything, yet now that I try to recall everything, I find that I can remember only certain things. I do know that I typed every word of these one hundred seventy-four pieces, not only typed, but retyped them. In those days I was a sloppy writer and had to copy everything after I had corrected the manuscript. All the typing was done on a Remington portable.

The journal records that I actually sold one hundred seven of the one hundred seventy-four pieces that I wrote during this twenty-two month period, but I hasten to add that I did not sell them immediately. A piece I may have written in August, 1932, may have sold as late as June, 1934.

The sale of one hundred seven pieces of a possible one hundred seventy-four may not seem discouraging, but bear with me through the sordid details.

Those one hundred seventy-four pieces consisted of every conceivable type of writing. Everything was grist, every avenue of publication was explored. Every type of writing that offered a buck was attempted. Nothing was too low, nothing too cheap.

I wrote Sunday School stories, I wrote spicy sex stories, I tried detective stories, sports stories, love stories. I wrote short-shorts and I even wrote a novel.

I wrote articles. Lord, I wrote articles! I sold one entitled "How to Eradicate Worms in Poultry." The *American Poultry Journal* paid me eight dollars for it. I wrote articles for salesmen's magazines, I wrote for writers' magazines. I reported an auction sale for a jewelry magazine. I wrote filler pieces for Sunday School papers, telling boys how to make money.

Since my first writing success had been with Sunday School papers, I banged out thirty-nine Sunday School stories, including six short serials. My success with them was less than spectacular. Although I eventually sold twenty-six of these stories, including three of the serials, I made the sales the hard way. Very few of the stories sold the first time out. They were rejected and rejected. Since the top rate in the field was only a half cent a word and many of these stories sold for as little as a seventh of a cent a word, my income from the Sunday School paper field was meager indeed. The stories, including the three serials, brought me only two hundred five dollars, an average of slightly more than a quarter of a cent a word.

Thirty-six pulp stories (most of these written in early 1934) came from the much-abused Remington. Only twelve of these sold for a total of one hundred fifty-six dollars and I never received payment for four. Tom

Wood of *Underworld* bought five of the stories. He paid me only twelve dollars and fifty cents. In 1934, when I was in New York, I made repeated attempts to collect from Old Tom, but he died, owing me forty-nine dollars and fifty cents.

Of the other pulp stories, one brought me thirty-five dollars. A short-short sold to *Phantom Detective* for seven dollars and fifty cents. The other stories, slanted for the pulps, were not sold to pulps. Rejected, I eventually unloaded them on cat-and-dog publications. One was snapped up by *Grit* for three dollars and fifty cents. It was a thirty-five hundred-word story and was "snapped up" after being rejected by twenty-two other publications. The postage involved in sending this story out twenty-three times was more than the amount received.

I had read somewhere of a writer having sold a thousand to two thousand short-shorts and I gave this type of story a workout. I produced sixteen straight short-short stories. I sold twelve. Only two were bought by the markets for which they were intended. King Features Syndicate bought one for six dollars and McClure's Syndicate took one for five dollars. The rest were disposed of to fraternal magazines, sometimes for as low as two-fifty or three dollars. The short-short venture netted me a grand total of fifty-two dollars and fifty cents.

Early in this period I knocked off a thousand-word story, entitled "Dice of Death." I submitted it to *Foreign Service*, which was listed in the *Writer's Digest* as paying two cents a word. I was stunned when they not only bought "Dice of Death" but actually sent me a check for twenty dollars on acceptance.

I promptly became a military expert and wrote sixteen more short-shorts, all with Army, Navy or Marine backgrounds.

Here I found my best market, word-wise. I actually sold sixteen of the seventeen stories, but, alas, only one more was taken by *Foreign Service*. Each, as it was written, was submitted to *Foreign Service*, but they all came back promptly. Next they went to *The Leatherneck*, the Marine publication which bought one story for five dollars. One was bought by *Our Navy* for the lowest price I ever received for a story, one dollar. Ten were taken by *Our Army*, but here the pay varied between two dollars and two dollars and fifty cents per story—on publication. I was still trying to collect for some of these when I arrived in New York in the summer of 1934. The final two Army short-shorts were bought by *American Defense* for around two dollars per story. My sixteen service stories, including the two fantastic twenty dollar sales, netted me precisely eighty-three dollars and twenty-five cents.

Now we come to my most successful category, the sales article. I wrote a really ambitious short story which I hoped to sell to *The Saturday Evening Post*. After it was rejected by *The Post*, and about a dozen other magazines along the line, I sent it to *Blade & Ledger*, a mail order magazine published in Chicago. They paid me twenty dollars for it. I promptly bombarded them with a couple of more stories, but they were rejected.

On a quick visit to Chicago, I met the editor and he suggested I try something for another publication they had called *Extra Money*. This went to house-to-house salespeople. I read a copy, wrote an article and they bought it—for twenty dollars, very good for a short article of only fifteen hundred words. I promptly began submitting further articles to *Extra Money*. They promptly and continuously rejected them. But there were other magazines in this field: *Opportunity, Specialty Salesman, How to Sell, Independent Salesman*. I sold one or two each to *Opportunity* and *Specialty Salesman*, four to *Independent Salesman* and twelve to *How to Sell*. The twelve straight sales to *How to Sell* resulted in my being offered the job of managing editor in April, 1933.

How to Sell was published in Mt. Morris, Illinois, and I journeyed there and became the managing editor—at twenty-five dollars a week, only one hundred dollars a week less than I had been making a year previously when the Depression caught up with me.

I remained in Mt. Morris for fourteen months and actually worked my way up to thirty dollars a week, then on July 1, 1934, I gave up a life of toil and went to New York to "become a writer."

*   *   *

Meanwhile—back at the portable Remington, in Webster Groves, Missouri.

In two final categories, I lumped numerous articles and stories as "miscellaneous." There are fifteen miscellaneous articles of which ten are recorded as having sold for a total of one hundred eight dollars. Two of these articles brought twenty dollars each. Of eight miscellaneous fiction stories, three sold.

While living in Mt. Morris, Illinois, I read Jack Woodford's *Trial and Error*. He made novel writing sound easy. I wrote one, a "serious" novel. After spending about twenty dollars in postage on it, I retired it.

The one hundred seven pieces of material sold during the twenty-two-month period between August, 1932, and June, 1934, earned me a grand total of eight hundred fifteen dollars!

The majority of the magazines to which I sold during this period paid on publication, which meant that I had to wait from three to six months for the money. I kept the stories humming through the mails. They came back as fast as I mailed them. Monday was always the crucial day. One Black Monday I had fourteen stories rejected. But another Great Monday I had five checks in the mail.

Weeks went by sometimes without a single sale. The postage bill was enormous. Of the eight hundred fifteen dollars earned during the period, a third of it must have been spent on postage. I had as many as forty stories in the mail at one time. No story was ever returned that I did not send it out again that very day.

* * *

The job in Mt. Morris was a miserable one. Twenty-five dollars a week was minimal pay, even in 1934. We had to pay thirty-six dollars a month for a furnished apartment; we had no car. Our recreation consisted of walking and you had to do this around the village square, for if you walked three blocks in a straight line you wound up in a cornfield.

I pounded the portable Remington in Mt. Morris. I pounded it every night and all day Sunday. By rigid economy I managed to amass the huge sum of one hundred five dollars. My wife agreed to "visit" her mother while I traveled to New York to become a professional writer. The "visit" of my wife was intended to be for only two or three weeks until I "got started" in New York.

The visit lasted seven months.

Chapter Three

There were in existence in 1934 some one hundred fifty pulp magazines. Street & Smith, which had been established in 1855, was possibly the most solid of all the pulp publishers. It was in its own six-story building at 79 Seventh Avenue, just above Fourteenth Street. The company put out around thirty-five magazines, including *The Shadow, Doc Savage, Detective Story, Love Story, Western Story, Sport Story, Wild West Weekly, Top Notch, Clues,* etc.

About a dozen editors rode herd on the magazines. John Nanovic was in charge of eight or ten, Frank Blackwell had *Detective Story* and *Western Story,* Daisy Bacon was for many years the guiding light of *Love Story,* and F. Orlin Tremaine was the editor of *Clues, Astounding Stories* and two or three others.

Away downtown was the Frank A. Munsey Company, established by the fabulous Frank Munsey in 1887. Among its stalwarts were *Argosy, All-Story* (a love story magazine) *Railroad Stories, Munsey's Magazine* and *Detective Fiction Weekly.* Howard Bloomfield was editor of *Detective Fiction*, but he was soon to leave to become editor of *Adventure*. He was replaced by Duncan Norton-Taylor. The famous *Argosy* was currently edited by Jack Byrne, although he was soon followed by Chandler Whipple.

Popular Publications had been in business only a few years, but already had a thriving group of some twenty or twenty-five magazines, including *Dime Detective*, *Dime Western*, *Operator #5*, *The Spider*, and soon the company purchased *Adventure*. Rogers Terrill was editor-in-chief of all of the magazines with the exception of *Adventure*, where Bloomfield held sole authority. Terrill's assistants were Mike Tilden, Ken White, Edythe Seims (soon to become Mrs. Steve Fisher), Charles Ingerman and Alden Norton.

Popular Publications was then, and is still, located at 205 East Forty-second Street.

At 144 West Forty-eighth Street was *Standard Magazines*, established in 1932 by Ned Pines, but already a very successful company. Leo Margulies was editor-in-chief of the entire string of magazines.

Dell Magazines was down on Thirty-fourth Street. I believe Cliff Dowdey was then the chief editor, but he left soon to return to Virginia, where he became Clifford W. Dowdey, the distinguished author of Civil War novels. His place was taken by Art Lawson.

Warner Publications was at 515 Madison Avenue. The company owned but three magazines, *Field & Stream, Ranch Romances* and *Black Mask*. Each was a distinguished magazine in its particular field.

Short Stories was at 9 Rockefeller Plaza. It was owned by William J. Delaney, who had just bought the magazine from Doubleday & Company, the book publishers. He later purchased *Weird Tales* also.

Magazine Publishers was at 67 West Forty-fifth Street. Aaron Wyn was the publisher and Harry Widmer the chief editor. The company put out about twenty-five magazines, including *Ten Detective Aces*, *Ace Detective*, *Ace Western*, *Ace Sports* and *Western Trails*.

In addition to these publishers there were perhaps a dozen other companies putting out pulp magazines, but most of the companies had only one, two or three titles and some of them paid extremely low rates. The Martin Goodman chain was just starting. The company later became very big but at this time they paid only a half cent a word for stories.

Louis Silberkleit had just started his first pulp magazine, *Double Action Western*, but paid only around a third of a cent a word for stories.

Fawcett Publications was in the process of moving to New York from Robbinsdale, Minnesota, where the company had built up a line of successful pulp magazines, but in transferring to New York the company discontinued most of the pulps and began putting out magazines like *True*. Fawcett was not, in 1934, a large pulp market.

These companies represented The Establishment as of July, 1934.

*   *   *

As an avid reader of *Writer's Digest*, *Writer's Monthly* and *Author & Journalist* before coming to New York, I knew all about the magazines, their authors, their rates of pay and something about the personalities of the editors.

The Ace of Aces, the goal of all pulp writers, was *Black Mask*. The elite of the elite were the *Black Mask* writers. They were followed by the writers of *Adventure*, *Short Stories*, *Argosy*, and *Detective Fiction Weekly*.

The prestige of these magazines wasn't determined necessarily by the rate of payment to authors. *Black Mask* was reputed to pay two cents a word to start, with a scale rising to around four cents a word. *Detective Fiction Weekly* and *Argosy* were said to pay Max Brand five cents a word and numerous writers received around three cents a word. For that matter, *Dime Western* and *Dime Detective*, although not rated with the elite, paid a few writers as high as three cents a word: Walt Coburn, Harry F. Olmsted and perhaps one or two more.

The base rate of pay at the majority of the pulp magazines was one cent a word. The fringe publishers paid less, but at Standard, Popular, Street & Smith and Munsey the usual pay was one cent a word.

The average pulp magazine of one hundred twenty-eight pages contained sixty-five thousand words. Since many of the magazines, such as *Argosy*, *Detective Fiction Weekly*, *Love Story*, *Western Story*, *Wild West Weekly*, were weeklies, the total market for stories was considerably greater than one hundred fifty times sixty-five thousand words.

There were also a number of semimonthly publications, such as *Ranch Romances* and *Short Stories*. Roughly, these weeklies and semimonthlies brought the total pulp market to about two hundred fifty copies of sixty-five thousand words per month. On a yearly basis some one hundred ninety-five million words were needed to fill the hungry maws of the pulps. At the base rate of one cent a word, this meant a total outlay of almost two million dollars per year for stories.

There were in and around New York some three hundred pulp writers who had made their marks and who descended periodically upon the several dozen editors to peddle their words. Perhaps another thousand established writers mailed in their wares from all parts of the country, and the world, for that matter. L. Patrick Greene, a regular contributor to *Short Stories*, lived in South Africa, and Max Brand, the king of kings of the pulps, had lived in Florence, Italy, for a dozen years. California alone boasted of no less than a hundred established pulp writers, including such giants as Erle Stanley Gardner, Walt Coburn and Harry Olmsted.

These twelve hundred to thirteen hundred pulp writers who made their livelihoods from writing for the pulps, some very good livelihoods, some meager, were by no means the entire competition in the pulp field. Nineteen thirty-four was still a Depression year and in the Depression there were literally thousands of people unemployed at their regular vocations, who turned to writing in the desperate hope that this might be the means of getting off WPA. Most of these were rank amateurs, but still many, many were gifted enough to sell an occasional story. They accounted for perhaps ten per cent of all the stories published in the pulps.

This was the world I had hoped to conquer when I arrived in New York on July 1, 1934.

My physical assets consisted of one portable Remington typewriter and my wardrobe which, aside from what I was wearing, fit very comfortably into one medium size suitcase. I had sixty dollars in cash, but paid out ten dollars and fifty cents of it for a week's rent in advance at the Forty-fourth Street Hotel. I squandered another ten dollars over the long weekend, so that on Tuesday morning, when I went out to size up the pulp jungle I had approximately forty dollars.

I had one thing else . . . the will to succeed.

Chapter Four

I got out of the bus depot on Forty-fourth Street and looking around saw the Forty-fourth Street Hotel, a few doors away. (Yes, this is the Forty-fifth Street Hotel in the Johnny Fletcher books and Room 821 where Johnny Fletcher and Sam Cragg always stay is the room I occupied for seven months.)

It was the Fourth of July weekend, so I could not really get around until Tuesday, when I called at the desk space "office" of a literary agent, Ed Bodin.

I first contacted Ed Bodin in 1933 while still living in Mt. Morris, Illinois. I sent him a story with a one dollar reading fee and he said it was pretty good and he would try it. The story didn't sell. I sent him about a half dozen more and early in 1934 was delighted when he sold a story to *Secret Agent X* for thirty-five dollars, which netted me twenty-eight dollars, for he charged a twenty per cent commission on the first five sales. I bombarded Ed with more stories, sending him, one, two and three a week. Each was accompanied by a reading fee of one dollar. Ed had twenty-two of these stories in his possession when I arrived in New York and these were the stories I was counting on to "get me started."

Not one of those twenty-two stories ever sold!

Ed Bodin's office was at 151 Fifth Avenue, just below Twenty-third Street. It was in a dingy loft building and he shared his office with five other persons. Each paid ten dollars a month for the use of a desk. There was only one phone in the room. When it rang, Ed Bodin and every one of the five office sharers dove for it.

The other desk space sharers of the office were, if I recall right, a private detective, a button broker, a dressmaker, a collection agent and a magazine publisher, Doc Levine. I listened many times to an impassioned sales pitch by the button broker as he tried to sell two dollars' worth of buttons to a dress shop, hoping to earn a fifty-cent commission.

The private detective waited hopefully for a twenty-five dollar divorce case where he could provide the "evidence" in the form of a professional corespondent.

Don't bother to use this group of colorful "desk space" boys as characters for a play. I started to write such a play in 1944 and called it "Desk Space." Steve Fisher was put on four weeks' layoff at RKO where we were both employed at the time. He thought he would write a book and not having a plot immediately, talked me out of this one, which I had all nicely laid out. He wrote the book in four weeks, called it *Winter Kill*. I was to get ten per cent if it sold to pictures and damned if he didn't sell it to Warner Brothers for twenty-five thousand.

Ed Bodin was a convivial man of about forty-five. On his letterhead he advertised: "Eleven Years with the Publishers of *Collier's, American Magazine*" etc. The letterhead did not say that he had worked in the circulation department of those magazines, not in the editorial. He was somewhat of a writer himself. He had actually sold a short-short story to the *New York Daily News* for twenty-five dollars and had photostatic copies of the story, which he liked to show to clients and prospective clients.

At one time or another, Ed Bodin had as clients, either as one dollar fee payers, or straight ten per centers, most of the writers whom I got to know in those days. He was an extremely likable man. He enjoyed society and gave many parties and went to all. He was well liked by the pulp writers and was ever ready to lend five dollars to needy writers. But only five dollars. Once you owed that you could get no more from him. However, in extremely grave circumstances, he would lend you ten dollars, but then you had to sign an IOU. I guess every writer in our group at one time or another borrowed five dollars from Ed and perhaps if the truth were known, all of them at one time or another tapped him for that emergency ten.

On that first visit to Ed Bodin's office, he took me across the street and introduced me to Arthur J. Burks. Before coming to New York I had read some adventure stories by Arthur J. Burks and looked forward to meeting him. He had been a Lieutenant in the United States Marine Corps during World War I and I visualized a lean, hard-bitten young man.

Instead of the John-Wayne-like type of man I had visualized, Arthur turned out to be a rather short man, weighing well over two hundred pounds and wearing thick glasses. He was thirty-six or thirty-seven. He was an amazingly fast typist and could compose stories as fast as he could type.

Later that year the New Yorker published a profile on Arthur in which they called him "The King of the Pulps" and in which Arthur was quoted as saying that a pulp writer who didn't make four hundred dollars a week wasn't worth his salt. This unfortunate remark caused Arthur some grief for there were few if any writers of the pulps who earned that much in 1934—and Arthur certainly did not make it, although he was capable of turning out as much as two hundred thousand words a month. However, writing two hundred thousand words a month and selling two hundred thousand words were entirely different matters.

On this day in New York I sat as a neophyte at the feet of the master. Arthur spent about three hours talking to me about the pulps and pulp writing, and one of the things he said made a profound impression upon me.

"The life of a pulp writer is seven years," Arthur said. "At the end of seven years you've got to go on to better writing, or go downhill."

I determined then and there that the pulps would have me for seven years—no more. In the meantime, I had to get the pulps . . . and I wasn't at all sure that they were waiting for me.

After lunch, I returned to Ed Bodin's office and met Steve Fisher. I had known him slightly by correspondence and he had arrived in New York from California only two weeks before I got to New York.

We hit it off and walked that afternoon down to Greenwich Village, where we sat in Washington Square for two or three hours, talking about our hopes, our dreams, our ambitions.

Later we strolled to Steve's apartment on Christopher Street. It wasn't a bad little apartment and contained a cot, a couple of chairs and an old piano. The floor was conspicuously rugless. While we were talking about the penthouses we would both have in the very near future, the door burst open and in charged a little lady who took one look at the rugless floor and lit into Steve with a choice vocabulary of four-letter words.

The Awful Truth came out. When Steve arrived in New York, penniless, he had come upon this apartment, which the lessor was trying to sublet. Steve had done a great sales job and had not only talked the little lady out of paying the rent in advance, but had gotten her to agree to let him send out the rug to be cleaned. Not only that, but the subleasing lady even gave him the six dollars to pay for the cleaning of said rug.

Now, two weeks later, the rug was still at the cleaners for Steve had eaten up the six dollars. That was the substance of the little lady's beef.

I felt terribly sorry for Steve's plight and even went across the street and picked up and paid for Steve's shoes which were being half-soled.

Chapter Five

By the use of the United States mails I had sold one short-short story to *Phantom Detective*, owned by Standard Magazines, for the sum of seven dollars and fifty cents.

Via the same United States mails, I had sold four stories to Tom Wood of *Underworld*, for a total of sixty-four dollars, but I had collected for only one of them at a quarter of a cent a word.

Through Ed Bodin, I had sold one story to *Secret Agent X*, owned by Rose Wyn, wife of Aaron Wyn of Magazine Publishers, but operating her own small pulp house a block from her husband's.

Until my arrival in New York, I had known only one person there, Ed Bodin.

Before coming to New York I had received a few bulletins (from Ed Bodin) about the American Fiction Guild, a national organization of pulp writers. Arthur J. Burks was the national President and Norvell Page, the head of the New York chapter. The AFG held a weekly luncheon at Rosoff's Restaurant on Forty-third Street.

From seventy-five to one hundred writers attended each luncheon. Arthur Burks sold me a membership at ten dollars, but I paid only two dollars down.

*   *   *

I spent Wednesday and Thursday making the rounds of the pulp editorial offices. I got in to see only two editors, Tom Wood of *Underworld* and Rose Wyn of *Secret Agent X.* Tom Wood was "bought ahead" on stories and could buy no more for several months.

Rose Wyn needed a five-thousand-word-story and asked me to write one. I did and it was rejected the next day.

All of the other editors were in conference, making up issues of magazines, etc. One or two sent out secretaries, who brushed me off.

On Friday, I went to the luncheon of the American Fiction Guild and met some of the successful pulp writers, as well as some medium successful writers and a few like myself who had sold one, two or three stories and were trying to storm the citadels.

Leo Margulies was the only editor at this first meeting of the luncheon of the American Fiction Guild. He was a crisp, outspoken man aged thirty-four, reputed to receive two hundred and fifty dollars a week. He was cordial, invited me to see him at his office.

Among the giants of the pulps I met at this luncheon, or in the next two or three weeks, were George Bruce, Norvell Page, Walter Gibson, Theodore Tinsley, Frederick C. Davis and Harry Sinclair Drago.

George Bruce was the ace of the air-war story writers

who was drawing down one and a half to two cents a word for his vast output of words. He was the first writer I knew who used an electric typewriter and sold virtually everything that he wrote.

Lester Dent was the creator and writer of the monthly *Doc Savage* novel, for which he drew down five hundred dollars a month, Norvell Page was writing *The Spider*, for which he received five hundred dollars a month, but soon boosted it to six hundred dollars, then seven hundred dollars. Frederick C. Davis wrote the monthly lead novel for *Operator #5*. Harry Sinclair Drago was very big in westerns and Theodore Tinsley wrote regularly for *Black Mask*.

Among the budding young writers I met that first week, or soon after, were L. Ron Hubbard (the man who later "invented" Dianetics), Charles Marquis Warren, Preston Grady, Paul Ernst, Arthur Leo Zagat and Mort Weisinger, who became one of my closest friends.

Many of the writers were still in their twenties, but I would say that the majority were in their thirties and a few in their forties and fifties, and even older. J. Allen Dunn came to many of the later meetings and he was in his late sixties. I also got to know Victor Rousseau very well later on, and he once told me that he had hunted lions in Matabeleland in 1889, so he must have been well in his sixties. Theodore Tinsley was a mild-mannered man of about forty who lived in the Bronx and was that rare article, a native New Yorker. His *Black Mask* character, Jerry Tracy, was a Broadway columnist, a frequenter of the night clubs and gay spots. I don't believe Ted Tinsley was ever inside a night club himself. He was an extremely conservative man, a plodding hard-working writer, not given to the frivolous things.

Lester Dent actually lived on a farm in La Plata, Missouri, but he came to New York two or three times a year and spent months there each time. He was a big, meticulous, redheaded man. He was the best gimmick and gadget creator who ever lived. He would have been terrific on the present-day tricks-and-gadget spy stories.

Lester was a bit of an adventurer and for several years owned a small yacht and went off frequently down to the Caribbean treasure hunting. He never found any. Lester lived well, but was awfully careful with the nickels and dimes. He passed on a few years ago, but I had a long conversation with him by phone just before his passing, when I telephoned him in Missouri about buying one of his old short stories for the television show, "Tales of Wells Fargo."

Lester was an extremely facile writer and craftsman, but was dissatisfied with his Doc Savage writing and tried to do better things. I believe he contributed only two stories to *Black Mask* in later years, which he rewrote and rewrote. He spent at least two years trying to crash the slick paper magazines and I believe he wrote twenty stories and finally sold one. He blamed his long years of pulp writing upon his inability to make the "big time."

However, he was big time with us younger writers

right from the start. He treated us as decently in those early years as he did later on, and both Steve Fisher and I talk about him fondly every now and then. When Steve became somewhat affluent in later years he bought an enormous Great Dane dog named Johnny.

Johnny was possibly the most widely traveled Great Dane that ever lived. Steve took him to France, later to Hollywood, but finally, in New York, he was told to dispose of the Great Dane by an unfriendly hotel manager. Lester had taken a liking to Johnny and offered Steve fifty dollars for him. As Lester was about to depart for Missouri, where Johnny would have living room, Steve sold Johnny to Lester. A few months later Steve was in Hollywood and thinking about Johnny, picked up the phone and called Lester in Missouri. He asked Lester to bring Johnny to the phone and have him bark.

Lester never quite got over that and mentioned the incident the last time I talked to him, about 1957.

I met Mort Weisinger at that first AFG luncheon. Mort was then a mere nineteen, but already a university graduate, taking a medical course at New York University. On the side he was operating a small literary agency for science fiction writers. Mort lived in Union City across the Hudson River, but came to New York City every day.

At the age of nineteen, Mort was one of the most brilliant persons I have ever known. Extremely erudite, he was an excellent writer of science fiction himself. Physically, Mort was six feet tall and weighed over two hundred twenty pounds; he later went up to three hundred but in recent years keeps his weight down to a trim (for him) two hundred fifty pounds.

I became very friendly with Jack Reardon, who was not a writer himself but had been with the American News Company for years and now had a job in the circulation department of the Vincent Astor-Raymond Moley political magazine, *Today* (later merged with *Newsweek*). Jack was a raconteur par excellence, possessed of a marvelous singing voice. He would frequently stop in at the Fourth-fourth Street Hotel in the evening before going home and the three of us, Jack, Mort Weisinger and myself would go out for a bite at Thompson's Restaurant around the corner on Sixth Avenue, across the street from the Hippodrome.

On the occasion of my first meeting with Steve Fisher I had felt terribly sorry for his plight, but within two weeks my own financial condition was as extreme as Steve's. I lived it up on those sixty dollars I had with me when I arrived in New York. I paid a week's rent in advance, then another week's and I ate three meals every day. It didn't matter; one of those twenty-two stories Ed Bodin had would sell any day. Or a new one that I was writing almost every day.

But the stories didn't sell. Desperately I made the rounds. I called on Standard Magazines, at Street & Smith, at Popular Publications, even away downtown at the Frank Munsey office. I called at the fringe pulp magazines, those paying a half cent a word.

I couldn't get in to see the editors. I carried my stories with me, but I had to hand them to secretaries and, now and then, an assistant editor.

The editors were seeing writers all the time, all day long. They were buying stories from writers each and every day. Every Friday at the Fiction Guild luncheon there were writers with checks; they showed them freely. Checks for fifty dollars, a hundred—sometimes even more.

Leo Margulies, editor-in-chief of Standard Magazine's thirty-five pulps, always came down to the American Fiction Guild luncheons, but his time was monopolized by the selling writers. I did, however, get to see him at his office, and he encouraged me to keep submitting stories to him.

They had a system at Standard Magazines that made it difficult for a beginner to break in. Leo himself did not read the stories. They were read by three different readers in the back office. If all three readers approved of the story, Leo purchased it automatically, but if one reader out of three said no, the story was rejected. Later, Leo explained the system to me and he encouraged me to write detective stories, love stories, adventure stores. I did—and they were all rejected.

Chapter Six

Our Army owed me for two stories that I had sold them while still living in Mt. Morris, Illinois. The stories had not yet been published, but needing money desperately, I decided to see if I could not get the five dollars that was due me for the two stories. I took the subway to Brooklyn and then walked about fourteen blocks to the offices of Our Army.

The editor was glad to see me until I broached the subject of the five dollars that was due me on publication for the two stories. He shook his head. The stories could not be paid for until they were published. I explained my financial condition. Sorry, he could not break the company's rule.

I walked back to the subway station, found that my total capital was now reduced to ten cents. I walked across the Brooklyn Bridge, hoofed it to Times Square. I squandered the ten cents on a meager lunch, then decided to brace Tom Wood of Underworld. He still owed me fifty dollars on those four pulp stories which had been published but not paid for.

He was on the telephone when I entered his office. I

sat down in a chair beside the desk and added up the amounts of the bets he was placing with his bookie. Fourteen dollars. This should be a cinch, I thought.

He got through placing his horse bets and I bluntly asked him if I could have the fifty dollars that was due me. I still remember the scene. He was in his shirt sleeves which were rolled up to his elbows. He was taking osteopathic treatments and something had gone wrong and his arms were covered with egg-size knobs. Tom, at this time, was probably in his sixties and had a quavering voice.

He did not really own the magazine, he told me quaveringly. *Underworld* was owned by a printer in Boston who gave him a monthly pittance for editing it. His poor old wife had recently been compelled to get a job so they could exist. He was terribly sorry, but he could not pay me the fifty dollars.

Twenty dollars? Ten . . . ? His quavering became worse. It was almost a sob. He just couldn't do it. (Yet he had been able to place fourteen dollars in horse bets.)

I came down. Five dollars would help me out tremendously. And, finally, could he spare me two dollars?

He couldn't, but as I rose to go, his shaking hands reached into a vest pocket.

"W-would this help you any?"

He had two quarters in his fingers.

I fooled him. I took the fifty cents.

Poor Old Tom died a year or two later. He still owed me forty-nine dollars and fifty cents.

*   *   *

I got an occasional small check from the old stories I had sold while still living in Mt. Morris. Two dollars, once in awhile, five dollars. Barely enough for food, not enough to pay my hotel rent. I had to do something to get myself known to the editors, to get my foot in those editorial doors.

The American Fiction Guild was having its annual election and I decided to run for secretary. Mort offered to campaign for me, although campaigning for such an office was an unheard-of thing.

I was already having my meals at MacFadden's Penny Restaurants (God bless Bernarr MacFadden). The restaurants are no more, but in those days you could dine sumptuously for around nine cents per meal. A hamburger steak made of meat-flavored sawdust cost four cents, a good, hard roll was a penny, coffee, two cents (made from dishwater with a dash of chicory) and dessert, two cents. You ate the meal standing up, which was good for your digestion. The food was very filling.

I had "tomato soup" at the Automat on Broadway at least once a day. The Automat restaurants, which are peculiar to the East, are just what the name implies. You get a flock of nickels from the cashier, then go down the battery of little cubicles, inside of which repose the articles of food that appeal to you. Pie, sandwiches, whatnot. In 1934 a sandwich was ten cents. You put two nickels into a slot, turned a knob and you were then able to open the little door and take out the sandwich.

There were a few things the inventors of the Automat were not able to lick, such as coffee and tea. You put a nickel into a slot, held a cup under a nozzle and got a cupful of black coffee. Sugar and cream, however, had to be on the table.

In the case of tea the problem was more complex. You could get a cup of hot water free, but you had to put a nickel into a slot to get a teabag.

So this is how the famous Automat tomato soup came into being. You got a bowl intended for soup, went over to the hot water nozzle and filled up your bowl. You sidled along to where you got the soup and picked up a couple of glassine bags of crackers (free), supposedly to go with the soup. You now went to one of the tables, sat down and crumbled the crackers into the hot water. Every table had a bottle of ketchup. You emptied about half of the ketchup into the hot water and cracker mixture. Presto—tomato soup!

Cost? Nothing.

I sometimes had tomato soup four or five times a day.

Jack Reardon introduced me to the Exchange Buffets and I gave them my patronage on those days when I was really hungry and had a dime. Unfortunately, the closest Exchange Buffet was on Fourth Avenue and Eighteenth Street, twenty-six blocks from the Forty-fourth Street Hotel. The long walk would whet my appetite even more.

The Exchange Buffet operated on the Honor System. You went from counter to counter, ordered everything you thought you could eat, then filled yourself to bursting and finally went up to the cashier just inside the door and told her the amount of your purchases. I ate some extremely good two-dollar meals there for ten cents.

Through the years I have received many, many letters from people who have tried to guess the real name of the hotel in which my fictional characters, Johnny Fletcher and Sam Cragg, always stay when they are in New York. In the books I call the hotel the Forty-fifth Street Hotel, but there is no such hotel. There was a Forty-fourth Street Hotel, which was later renamed the King Edward Hotel. It is at 120 West Forty-fourth Street.

Quite a few of my readers have guessed the identity of the hotel and a few have sent me pictures of it. Now and then I even get a letter from someone who tells me that they have asked for, and occupied, Room 821, in which I lived for seven months. These readers, however, know the room only because of my stories. They do not know that I personally waged a six-and-one-half-month cold war with the manager of the Forty-fourth Street Hotel.

In the Johnny Fletcher books I call the manager Mr. Peabody and describe him as a tart-tempered little man. The real manager was entirely different. He was a big man with a booming voice and the disposition of a wounded grizzly bear. I guess in those early years after leaving the Forty-fourth Street Hotel I created a mental block to forget this hotel manager's name, for I cannot for the life of me now recall it. It was something like Wagenheim. All Times Square hotel managers are tough. They have to be, but I am willing to back Mr. Wagenheim against any or all of them. He was T-O-U-G-H.

The only edge I had on Wagenheim was that I could spend my full time thinking how to outwit him, whereas he had to run a hotel and could only spend a certain amount of time figuring out how to beat the sharpies, deadbeats and whatnots who stayed at the hotel.

In 1934 there were no tourists visiting New York and if there had been they would not likely have chosen a hostelry such as the Forty-fourth Street Hotel. The people who lived there were broken-down actors, starving actors, hungry vaudevillians, wrestlers, poor opera singers, touts, bookies, sharpies, hungry actors, no, I said that before, and all-around no-goods and deadbeats. And one hungry, would-be writer.

I will say this for Mr. Wagenheim: during that long, bitter cold war he never stopped calling me MISTER Gruber. But the tone of voice he used made that MISTER an epithet.

The elevators were right alongside the desk and you could hardly get into one without being seen. I would come sidling into the hotel, keeping close to the wall, and dart into the first elevator. As I stepped or leaped in I would hear the voice, loud and clear and rasping: "MISTER Gruber!"

But I was hard of hearing and went up to Room 821. The phone would be ringing. I would try ignoring it, but there was no use. I would answer. "MISTER GRUBER," snarled Mr. Wagenheim, "would you please come downstairs?"

The man had a one-track mind. He wanted the rent. He once boasted to me that no one had ever gotten into him for more than three weeks' rent and he actually told me another time—which I used in the first Johnny Fletcher book—"A bishop once occupied Room 821. He stayed there for three weeks and didn't pay his rent. I locked him out on the twenty-second day."

I am proud to say that I broke the long-established record. I actually got into the hotel for six weeks' rent.

In the early days I ate in the hotel dining room and charged the meals to my room. Wagenheim cut off my credit after I owed the hotel two weeks' rent. The dining room, unfortunately, did not do a very good business.

I have mentioned that I was a candidate for secretary of the American Fiction Guild. I passed on this information to Mr. Wagenheim, but I told a small fib. I told him that I was elected. Actually, I was defeated.

As secretary of the AFG, I told Mr. Wagenheim, I could have the writers use the dining room of the Forty-fourth Street Hotel for their weekly luncheons— seventy-five to a hundred writers at fifty cents a plate.

He was delighted with the idea and I got by the third week. He nailed me the next week, however, and I told him I was having a bit of trouble with the executive committee; they liked the meals we were now getting at the Knickerbocker Hotel and were afraid those of the Forty-fourth Street Hotel wouldn't come up to the Knickerbocker standard.

That was a challenge to Mr. Wagenheim. "Bring over your executive board for a sample lunch. On the house, of course."

I brought over Steve Fisher, Mort Weisinger, Jack

44

Reardon and two other starving writers and we had such a meal as the boys (and myself) hadn't had in many weeks. We told the manager that his grub had it all over that of the Knickerbocker.

I got through the fifth and sixth weeks with this "sample" lunch and then Mr. Wagenheim played dirty pool. He checked up and found out that I had been defeated in my bid for the secretaryship of the AFG. He put the French Key in my door that night.

The French Key is a little instrument invented by a ghoulish hotel manager. It is a key made of extremely soft metal. It is inserted in the lock, twisted and broken off. Then try to get into the room and sneak out your luggage and typewriter. When the French Key has accomplished its purpose the hotel management forces a sharp, pointed key into the soft metal key stub, turns it and pulls out the French Key with ease . . . but since starving writers never possess the withdrawal key, the French Key is quite effective.

I spent the night riding the subway, back and forth, back and forth, and in the morning I walked down to Ed Bodin's office and borrowed that emergency ten dollars, which got me back into the Forty-fourth Street Hotel.

Chapter Seven

In late August, or early September, a windfall came along. William B. Ziff, president of the Ziff-Davis Company of Chicago, had opened a New York office. Ziff's father had built up a successful business in Chicago as advertising representative for most of the Negro newspapers throughout the country.

Ziff, Jr., inherited the business, but wanted to expand and took in B. G. Davis to establish a group of magazines which eventually became quite successful. Ziff, however, liked better the cosmopolitan atmosphere of New York. Someone sold him an idea for a new magazine which, purporting to be an expose of gambling and sharpshooters, was actually intended to give the reader of the magazine an edge in games of chance.

Ed Bodin was chosen to be the editor of this magazine. This was great news for Ed Bodin's clients and those boys of the American Fiction Guild who needed a few dollars to tide them over.

I devoted most of my time for about a month gathering data and writing eight articles for Ed Bodin. I was paid for each article as I delivered it and earned altogether around eighty dollars for the eight articles. I "exposed" the numbers game, the wire houses, the floating crap games of New York (of which I knew absolutely nothing). The magazine was called *Doc Wizard's Lucky Systems*. Only the one issue was published for it was a colossal flop, but that eighty dollars helped me tremendously.

I was very flush that month and because of it, I got into a cold war with science fiction writers that exists, to a degree, to this very day.

I have mentioned that Mort Weisinger had a small agency for science fiction writers. He charged a one-dollar reading fee for stories and took ten per cent from any sales that he made—which were few and far between. I doubt if he averaged more than five or six dollars a week from this business. A ten-dollar week was a big week for Mort.

A staggering thing happened to Mort during this same month that I was cleaning up at *Doc Wizard's Lucky Systems*. A science fiction writer in Milwaukee had mailed Mort a sixty thousand–word novel. Mort submitted it to *Astounding Stories* and went around later to pick it up. To his astonishment he was handed a check for twelve hundred dollars. They were buying the novel at two cents a word.

Mort had never seen twelve-hundred-dollar checks before. In his wildest dreams he had never expected to earn one hundred twenty dollars from a single sale. He had, in fact, no bank account into which to deposit the check.

We kidded the life out of Mort. We told him he

would probably never see twelve hundred dollars again in his entire lifetime and to take the money and skip to Argentina with it. We suggested other things he could do with the money. At least he could *stall* sending the money to Milwaukee.

Mort was an honest lad, however, and after carrying the check around for a week or so, he opened a bank account and when the check cleared he sent the money to Milwaukee, minus his one hundred twenty dollars' commission.

With such a huge sum in the bank, Mort now began talking up science fiction and science fiction writers. Jack Reardon was in my room at the Forty-fourth Street Hotel to go with me to the luncheon of the American Fiction Guild when Mort came in with his understudy in science fiction, Julius Schwartz. With Julius aiding and abetting him, we got into an argument about pseudoscience fiction and pseudoscience fiction writers. I had Jack Reardon on my side and when you had Jack with you, you didn't need anyone else.

In the heat of the discussion I made the statement that all pseudoscience writers were weirdies. I was roundly denounced by both Mort and Julius and in the ensuing melee I came out with the flat declaration that I could pick out a pseudoscience writer in a roomful of people.

Mort promptly challenged me. J. Hamilton Edwards was in New York from his home upstate and would be at the American Fiction Guild. Mort had ten dollars that said I could not pick J. Hamilton Edwards out of the crowd on sight.

I was raised on my own petard and couldn't back down. But I reduced the bet from ten dollars to two. Mort insisted that we not go to the luncheon until everyone else would already be there.

We finally got to the luncheon. Some sixty or seventy writers were seated in the dining room. Mort looked around and declared: "J. Hamilton Edwards is here. I defy you to pick him out on sight."

My eyes went around the U-shaped luncheon table. They came to rest on one lad with buck teeth as big as those of Clement Atlee's son-in-law.

I pointed. "That is J. Hamilton Edwards."

It was.

The story got around and the science fiction writers still hate me.

A year or two ago I came across a new book by J. Hamilton Edwards, who has gone along and is quite famous in his field. It had a picture of him on the back cover. The buck teeth are gone!

Modern dentistry is wonderful.

You will note that in the foregoing episode I have used the term "pseudoscience fiction." That is what it was called in 1934 and for years before and after. Since the War, however, the "pseudo" has been dropped.

The term was a rather broad one to begin with. It included "science" stories, fantasy, tales of monsters and werewolves.

Chapter Eight

The weeks rolled on. I *existed*. Some days I had a single meal, some days I tasted no food at all other than the tomato soup at the Automat. Sometimes I ate only tomato soup three days running.

If you will turn back the pages you will find mention of some articles I sold to *Independent Salesman* back in 1932, while I was sweating it out in Webster Groves, Missouri. The magazine paid on publication and needing the money at the time, I wrote them my wolf letter with which I had regaled a number of publishers and which had even now and then turned the trick.

The letter was something about the wolf howling at my door every night for two weeks, but now, alas! the wolf had stopped howling. The reason: I had sneaked out of the house, caught the wolf, throttled him with my bare hands, then skinned and sold the pelt. The proceeds had enabled me to eat for a few days, but the word had gotten around among the wolves and they no longer came and howled. In short, I needed money something fierce and would the kind publisher send me the check now instead of waiting to pay on publication, because then my heirs might benefit, but not me. I would have starved to death.

Independent Salesman owed me thirty dollars for two articles. Upon receipt of the wolf letter they came through nobly, sending me by air mail a check for twenty-seven dollars and fifty cents, with a note saying that they didn't mind saving me from starvation, but business was business and instead of the thirty clinkers, only twenty-seven dollars and fifty cents. I saw no fault in that and cashed the check and bought the wherewithals of life.

Three months later (and the wolves were howling louder than ever) *Independent Salesman* came out carrying both of my paid-for articles in a single issue. In the same mail was a check for thirty dollars, payment for the pieces. Letter, signed Marty Siegel, Editor.

I debated with my conscience for about eight hours, then mailed the check back, saying that I had already been paid. The decision to return the check was simply because I figured they would learn of the mistake themselves and write me in a few days, demanding the thirty bucks, or gendarmes.

A note came from Marty Siegel. I was an honest lad, of which there weren't many. Not much more said about it.

Comes now early winter, or late fall of 1934. I am sitting in the Forty-fourth Street Hotel about two o'clock of a Sunday afternoon. I am thinking of the lunch I haven't had, the breakfast I missed, the dinner of the night before, and the lunch of the day before that I also didn't eat. In other words, I was thinking of food and wishing that I had a few thin dimes to purchase same.

A knock on the door.

It couldn't be Mr. Wagenheim; he had threatened me only that morning. What could I lose? I opened the door. A giant stood in the doorway. He was lean of waist, broad of shoulder, about six-four. Swarthy. He could have passed for a member of Murder, Inc.

"Frank Gruber?" he demanded in a half-snarl.

A bill collector? Don't make me laugh. I was bill collector proof. A holdup? I would help him search and ask only ten per cent of what he found.

He brushed past me into the room, in which there was space to swing a cat lengthwise, but not crosswise. He looked around, whirled on me.

"I always wanted to see how a starving writer lived," he said. Then suddenly he could carry it on no longer, stuck out his hand, grabbed mine and said: "I'm Aron Mathieu of Cincinnati."

He was the editor of the *Writer's Digest*, which also published the sales magazine, *Independent Salesman*. He was in New York on business and sitting in his hotel on Sunday had thought of me and making a few phone calls, had located me—through Arthur J. Burks.

Hold on!

For two years he had thought of me every now and then and wondered what sort of duck I was. All because of that thirty-dollar check I had returned to his company in 1932! He swore roundly even then that I was the only downright honest writer he had ever heard of. He insisted that no writer on earth, especially one who was as close to the howling wolves as my letter had indicated, would have done such a thing. So that was why he was now visiting me.

He had a proposition, but first of all, why not step out, go down the street to Schrafft's and have a bite of lunch? I was out of the door before he had half of the word "lunch" out of his mouth.

We had lunch and then went back to the hotel and he visited with me for about three hours.

The proposition? He was going to bring out a year book, the first of what became a very famous annual publication, still coming out every year. He wanted to have a list of the literary markets compiled for the magazine and thought he ought to have someone in New York who knew his way around do the job. He would pay me fifty dollars for it and he was sure the work wouldn't take me more than a week.

I accepted while still at lunch, but mellowing afterwards, Aron said that he would like to have a really bang-up job and maybe fifty wasn't enough. How about seventy-five dollars?

When a pigeon comes into a hungry tomcat's lair, it is only natural that the pigeon have a bite taken out of him, so I said, well, a really bang-up job ought to be worth maybe a hundred.

For a moment I thought Aron would forget those kind thoughts he had had of me since 1932, but he held himself in beautifully and we compromised on ninety bucks and then he reached into his pocket and pulled out two twenties and said, "Here's an advance and next week when I get back to Cincinnati I will send you the other fifty. I know you will deliver."

I have, since 1934, had in my hands a number of checks of five figures, and the checks had my name on them, but the thrill was not as great as that magnificent day in 1934, shortly after a sumptuous lunch, when I held in my hand forty bucks. Cash!

Chapter Nine

It is time I drew a fullscale portrait of Steve Fisher. While I was still editor of *How to Sell* in Mt. Morris, Illinois, Steve sent me a short story, as we occasionally bought one for very low rates. I didn't buy Steve's story, but we wrote several letters back and forth. He told me that he was going to New York early in June and I told him that I, too, had the idea buzzing around in my bonnet.

Steve got to New York just two weeks before my own arrival. I met him in Ed Bodin's office on my first visit there, and we hit it off immediately.

I went down to the Village several times during the next two or three weeks and he took me around. In those few weeks he had lived in the Village he had gotten to know a surprisingly large number of the denizens.

When he arrived in New York, Steve was twenty-one or twenty-two, although already a veteran of a four-year hitch in the United States Navy. He was a Californian and had spent most of his boyhood in boarding schools.

At the age of sixteen he had run away from the last boarding school and enlisted in the Navy.

He began writing while in the Navy and sold some stories to *U.S. Navy* and *Our Navy*. When he came out of the Navy he lived in Los Angeles and tried to crash the New York fiction markets. He found it an exceedingly difficult task. He sold a few stories to *U.S. Navy* for something like a tenth of a cent a word. He wrote for the sex magazines, now and then, and he sold a single pulp story to *Top Notch Magazine* edited by F. Orlin Tremaine. I believe he also sold one short-short story to the *Thrilling* group, and he sold a couple to Leo Margulies after his arrival in New York and then the editorial doors seemed to close in his face.

Since I had myself left home at the tender age of sixteen and enlisted in the United States Army, Steve and I had this one thing in common. Otherwise, we both had the burning desire to succeed as writers.

Our lives since 1934 have been strangely parallel, careerwise. Our personalities, however, are vastly different. Yet there has been a tremendously strong bond between us through the years and a loyalty to one another possibly unparalleled among writers.

In those early days in New York there were writers and editors in New York who would say to me: "Steve'll never make the grade." Always I told them that they were wrong. I felt that Steve's tremendous ambition, his burning intensity would carry him through to success.

I am sure Steve heard criticism of me and defended

me in turn. Once when we were both established in *Black Mask*, I was out of town and a writer who thought he was already a great success since he had published a few books, was in the office and criticized one of my stories. Steve started a furious verbal war with him which reached such proportions that the editor threw the other writer out of the office and he became *persona non grata* with *Black Mask*.

Although our writing backgrounds are very similar, Steve and I write totally different styles and through the years our writing has been directed into different channels.

Steve's forte is romance. I have maintained through the years that no better writer exists than Steve when it comes to writing a scene between a man and a woman.

After his apprenticeship in the pulps, Steve began writing slick stories and has appeared in *Collier's*, *Liberty*, *Cosmopolitan*, *This Week*, etc. His stories have been highly regarded but I still believe his finest work was a pulp short story entitled "Goodbye Hannah." This story has been widely reprinted through the years.

Steve can write excellent mysteries when he sets himself to it. His novel, *I Wake Up Screaming*, was extremely successful as a book and was made into a very fine motion picture.

Those first few months in New York were bitterly cruel on Steve. He could not catch on. He was evicted from his first Greenwich Village apartment, then got three months' credit in a five-story walkup. The manager was a former Navy man and for that reason decided to give Steve the credit. The apartment was virtually unrentable, anyway.

One afternoon I climbed the stairs and found Steve writing a letter to the electric company. He let me read it. It was an impassioned plea to the company not to turn off his electricity. How would the electric light company feel, Steve asked, if they had turned off the electricity on Jack London? Well, he was going to be as big a success one day and the electric light company would be ashamed of itself.

The cold-hearted electric light company did not give a damn about Jack London, or Steve. The next time I went to see Steve he had only candlelight.

Steve was evicted from his second apartment the day before Christmas of 1934. With a typewriter under one arm, a suitcase under the other, he trudged the streets, block by block. He finally found a landlord who was willing to take a chance on him without a down payment on the rent.

Steve HAD to succeed. There was nothing else ahead for him but success.

*   *   *

It was Steve Fisher who introduced me to The Poets. Showing me the sights of Greenwich Village shortly after my arrival in New York, Steve led me one evening into a cellar in the basement of a tenement. The room was about twenty by thirty feet in size. Planks were laid on barrels, making a long table. Additional boards were laid on empty nail kegs, forming seats. There was no other furniture in the cellar.

Around this table were gathered The Poets. The street door that led down to the cellar had a scrawled notice on it: "The Village Vanguard."

There is today a famous place in Greenwich Village, The Village Vanguard. It is a large, very successful night spot that provides off-Broadway plays, musical reviews and dispenses dinners, liquors and whatnot. It is owned and operated by Max Gordon, the same Max Gordon who ran the 1934 cellar Vanguard for The Poets. The big tourist place of today was founded upon the original plank and barrel hideout of 1934.

Several years before coming to New York, I had come across a book, *Tramping on Life*. It was the autobiography of Harry Kemp. It was published about 1920 and told of Kemp's youth, of his wanderings and finally his descent upon New York. It was a fascinating book and gave a picture of the artist's life in New York that instilled in me a yearning for a similar life. More than anything else, Harry Kemp's book influenced me in the ultimate decision to go to New York and lead the Literary Life. I had this yearning from about 1927 or 1928, until my actual invasion in 1934.

And who was one of the first poets I met in the Village Vanguard?

Harry Kemp.

Harry Kemp, around 1920, reminisced of his own days in New York, circa 1910–1911. He had drawn a colorful, glamorous portrait of a way of life.

Now, in 1934, Harry Kemp was still leading the same life he had lived twenty-four years before. As I got to know Greenwich Village and The Poets, a slow horror built up in me.

These poets were an unwashed, unkempt, unwholesome lot. Their existence was tenuous, appalling. That there is no money in writing poetry everyone knows. Even the great Victorian poets had to depend on patrons for their very livelihood.

The existence of the Greenwich Village poets was a precarious one. And I am speaking of the upper echelon of poets, not the scrabbling would-be, untalented versifiers.

At The Village Vanguard night after night were poets who were famous even then, who today are in all the anthologies of great poetry.

Eight or ten of them would rent a bare, unfurnished room for about three dollars a week. Each contributed his thirty or forty cents. Some had an extra shirt which they washed themselves on rare occasions. They never wore ironed shirts.

They made the rounds of the Greenwich Village taverns and bars in the early evening hours. They recited their poems. Most of them had developed excellent voices and they would declaim in ringing tones. Patrons of the bar would sometimes toss them coins. The Poets cadged drinks. If they worked diligently of an evening they earned as high as forty or fifty cents—and got themselves a good snootful.

I was in the bar around the corner from The Vanguard one evening when a poet, famous then, today in almost every anthology, came in. He recited one of his excellent poems. A couple of pennies hit the floor, a nickel gave off a solid ring. The poet's eyes fastened on it as he continued to declaim.

The melodious tinkle of a dime brought a gasp from the poet. He broke off his declamation and made a headlong dive to the floor to snatch up the precious coin.

Later I visited The Village Vanguard and the same poet recited his poems to a smaller, more appreciative audience, albeit a non-paying one.

The Poets tolerated Steve Fisher and me. They criticized us freely and openly, calling us (at the least) commercial writers. Other times they sneered that we were selling our souls to Mammon.

Well, I guess we were trying to sell our souls but Mammon wasn't buying.

Chapter Ten

July, 1934.

August.

September.

October.

November.

I was making the rounds. I was getting past the secretaries, even the assistant editors, and I was getting to talk to the editors themselves. I got to know John Nanovic of Street & Smith, Duncan Norton-Taylor of *Detective Fiction Weekly*, Leo Margulies of Standard, Rogers Terrill of Popular, Harry Widmer of Magazine Publishers.

I submitted stories to all of them. I wrote at least forty stories during those months and all, all were rejected.

An astonishing thing happened to Mort Weisinger. He got a job at Standard Magazines and he began to talk up my stories in the back room. But he couldn't get two other readers to approve my stories. In the front office, Leo Margulies was getting very friendly, very sympathetic.

The boys in the back room didn't like my detective stories, they didn't like my love stories or my adventure stories. Early in December, Leo suggested I try a western story—the only type of story I had not written up to this time. He even gave me a copy of *Thrilling Western* to read.

I read the magazine from cover to cover and that evening sat down and pounded out two short-shorts entitled "Treasure Trap and Six-Shooters at Sundown." They were sixteen hundred and eighteen hundred words in length respectively.

I submitted them to Leo Margulies.

A couple of days later I got a surprising call from Rogers Terrill. I had heard of these things happening, but up to this time no one had ever called me.

It was Friday afternoon. They were going to press the next day, Saturday, and needed a fifty-five-hundred-word story to fill out the issue of *Operator #5*. Could I write a fifty-five-hundred-word story overnight? I could, I solemnly assured Rogers.

I sat down at the typewriter. By eight o'clock I had created Captain John Vedders of Military Intelligence. All I had to do now was figure out how he could save the world.

By ten o'clock I had come up with Leone Montez, the beautiful spy who was working for the "mysterious power" that was threatening the safety of every man, woman and child in the United States.

I still needed a plot.

By twelve o'clock I still needed a plot.

At two A.M. I had Captain John Vedders of Military Intelligence and the beauteous Leone Montez, the Panamanian spy.

All I needed was a plot.

At three-thirty, the entire United States Atlantic Fleet was about to be attacked by a fleet of bombers originating in a country in Europe. The beautiful Leone Montez had stolen the plans of the fleet maneuvers from a United States Naval Officer and was offering them for sale to the representative of the foreign power, who had a mysterious radio in the Catskills, from which the radio message would go to Europe, that would loose the bombers that would seek out the individual targets—pinpointed on the maneuver chart.

All Captain John Vedders had to do now was find the beautiful Leone Montez and get the stolen plans from her.

Unfortunately, however, the dastardly villain had mistrusted Leone Montez. He had abducted her, along with the plans, taken her to the hideout in the Catskills where he would hold her until he radioed his people in Europe.

All Captain John Vedders had to do was to find the hideout, get in, kill the villains and retrieve the stolen maneuver plans.

He found the hideout, all right, but the dastardly villains had an eight-foot, close-meshed fence all around the place and the fence was charged with about four thousand volts of A.C. electric current.

The villains had overlooked only one little thing.

They hadn't checked up on Captain John Vedders sufficiently. They didn't know that he had been the pole-vaulting champion of West Point.

It was a fatal mistake.

Captain John merely uprooted a little old tree, trimmed off the branches and pole-vaulted neatly over the electrically-charged fence.

And just in time, too.

The radio operator was already tapping out his message to the mysterious power in Europe. The bombers waited—they kept on waiting.

By eight o'clock in the morning all fifty-five-hundred words were down on paper, eighteen pages. There was no time to retype. I delivered the story at nine o'clock.

Noon.

No word from Rogers Terrill.

Monday.

No word from Rogers Terrill of *Operator #5*.

Tuesday.

Leo Margulies of Standard Magazines phoned. They were buying both "Treasure Trap" and "Six-Shooters at Sundown" for sixteen dollars and eighteen dollars respectively!

Flushed by this success, I went down to see Rogers Terrill.

"We don't pay until Friday," he said laconically.

Pay?

I just wanted to know about my story, "Murder Maneuvers." What had been wrong with it?

What had been wrong with it? Nothing. It was al- .

ready on the press. Good story. Do me another for next month.

He'd forgotten to call me on Saturday.

This was December 14, 1934.

I was "in."

Chapter Eleven

The tide turned that quickly. I wrote three westerns for Standard Magazines during the next month and all were accepted. I wrote another story for *Operator #5* and it, too, was bought.

The fluke that had gotten me into *Operator #5* was virtually repeated within a few weeks. I encountered Harry Widmer on the subway. I told him the details of my breaking into *Operator #5*. He said he had a similar situation. They were closing *Ace Sports* the next day and needed a forty-five-hundred-word story to fill the issue. I promptly volunteered to write it. We discussed the sport that I would write about and decided upon pole vaulting—of which I knew absolutely nothing.

I delivered the forty-five-hundred-word story, "Vault of Victory," and Harry Widmer confided in me that they were looking for two or three "novelette" western writers who would do ten-thousand-word stories for eighty-five dollars—fifteen per cent less than a cent a word.

I would be happy to be one of those novelette writers, I told Harry. I wrote one and he bought it.

It was now February and my back rent was paid up and I was very prosperous. It was time for my wife to end her "visit" with her mother and she came on to New York. She did not like the hotel and neither did I, after all the travail I had suffered in it.

My wife found an apartment on One Hundred and Tenth Street. Sixty-seven dollars a month. I signed the lease and we were scheduled to move in on March 1.

We went down to a "shofel" furniture house, picked out three hundred sixty dollars worth of furniture and I paid down thirty-six dollars—ten per cent, which was all the store asked for.

On February 28, I was informed by the store that they had investigated me and because I was "unemployed" they could not let me have the furniture for only ten per cent down. A free-lance writer? That didn't count as employment.

One hundred dollars additional or no furniture. I had submitted a story to Street & Smith that week and wonder of wonders, John Nanovic told me he was buying it. The check came the next day and with what I had, I managed to pay the hundred dollars to the shofel furniture house.

I had four markets now, Standard, Street & Smith, Popular and Magazine Publishers. I was writing a story a month for *Operator #5* and added to it a story a month for *The Spider*. Standard Magazines was taking at least two stories a month from me, as was Magazine Publishers.

My income from writing in 1934 had been less than four hundred dollars. That included the money from the three pulp stories I sold in December, the eighty dollars I had made from *Doc Wizard*, the ninety dollars from the *Writer's Digest* and the few checks that dribbled in from the cat-and-dog magazines to which I had sold stories prior to coming to New York.

My income in 1935 was ten thousand dollars. And that was very, very good money. In 1935, the late Franklin D. Roosevelt had been in office for two years and the country had already had the benefit of the NRA, the CCC, the WPA and the myriad of alphabetic governmental agencies that were supposed to aid industry, business and the worker. Yet to all intents and purposes the Big Depression was still as deep as it had been in the late Hoover days. A million or two "workers" had been absorbed into Federal work projects but seemed to have made no impression upon the unemployment statistics. These eleven or twelve million employed got exceedingly low wages.

But if wages were low in 1934 and 1935, so was the cost of living, and the young writers and would-be writers whom I knew were taking full advantage of it.

You could get a furnished room at five or six dollars a week. An apartment, of sorts, cost little more. I moved into the Forty-fourth Street Hotel when I first arrived in New York and got into the hole so quickly that I had to remain on whether I liked it or not. I paid (or owed) ten dollars and fifty cents for a fairly large room. The hotel had smaller rooms for nine dollars a week. In our circles, ten dollars and fifty cents a week for lodging was considered high. It was high for me, but I couldn't move because I owed too much.

You could get a room or apartment in Greenwich Village for much less. I knew several writers in the Village who had "apartments" that cost them only twenty-five dollars or thirty dollars a month. Fifty a month for an apartment was living it up.

Your food did not cost more than ten dollars a week and you ate well. A breakfast at Nedick's, the famous orange juice stands, cost ten cents. For that you got a small glass of orangeade, two doughnuts and a cup of coffee. Lunch at most of the mid-town restaurants was forty-five to fifty cents; dinner seventy-five cents to a dollar. If you were hard up, or ingenious, you could eat for much less. Thompson's on Sixth Avenue had two pork chops, coffee and the regular side dishes and bread for thirty cents.

The apartment we moved into on March 1, 1935, consisted of three rooms. It was in one of the better buildings on the upper West Side and we were really splurging. Two years later I bought a Buick automobile for seven hundred forty dollars. It was a large, heavy car, much more sturdily built than the flimsy things that pass today and cost seven times as much. I bought a Cadillac in 1941 which I drove throughout the war and for several years afterwards. It was a tremendously well-built machine, and I am sure the materials in it were better than you get today. The car cost me sixteen hundred dollars! Compare that with the eight thousand dollar Cadillacs of today.

You could buy shoes at Thom McAn's for three dollars and fifty cents. A suit of clothing at Bond's was twenty dollars.

A subway ride was a nickel.

The Roxy Theater on Seventh Avenue was one of the finest theater showcases in the world. You could see the top motion pictures, plus an hour stage show for thirty-five cents, up to six in the afternoon. The evening price was only fifty-five cents. The smaller Broadway theaters and the neighborhood cinemas cost between twenty-five and forty cents, for double bills.

There were many parties in our group. Writing being the lonesomest job in the world, the writers seized upon every occasion to throw parties, or to attend all to which they were asked.

The parties were gin parties. I gave one at our apartment on West One Hundred Tenth Street to which I invited some sixty persons. The total cost of the party was under ten dollars. I served only Tom Collinses (as did the other party givers). The cost was about eight dollars for the gin, a dollar for the ice and about fifty cents for the lemons. No food was expected at the parties.

The writers (and their wives) could really get drunk on that gin. One of the convivial editors who attended all parties always passed out at eleven o'clock in the evening. We would roll him over to one side of the room and continue with the party.

Inviting an editor to a party was a risk. It was fine to have him come to the party because it gave you a chance to get really acquainted with him, but there was always the chance that a writer who had had a story rejected by him was quite likely, with the gin to loosen his inhibitions, to pick a fight with the editor.

Leo Margulies was reputed to be the highest paid pulp editor in the business, drawing down two hundred fifty dollars in salary—enormous pay for those Depression years. He had been hired by Ned Pines because he knew every author in New York. He had been an office boy for Frank Munsey, then started a literary agency which serviced the Munsey magazines. Ned Pines was barely out of college when he started his chain of magazines. He needed a man who knew both stories and authors.

However, if Leo was the highest paid pulp editor, his assistants were among the lowest paid. I don't believe there was one of them who received more than thirty dollars a week. Mort Weisinger's starting salary there was only fifteen dollars a week.

As editor of a baker's dozen of the Street & Smith magazines, John Nanovic was responsible for the purchase of thousands of dollars' worth of manuscripts every month. Yet I don't believe his salary was ever higher than sixty-five dollars a week. His assistants received between thirty dollars and forty dollars a week. John was still a bachelor in 1935 and lived at the Taft

Hotel on Times Square. His room was about half the size of mine at the Forty-fourth Street Hotel. He paid nine dollars a week for it. The Munsey editors received between fifty dollars and seventy-five dollars a week, but by a series of dismissals and resignations, an assistant rose to be editor of *Detective Fiction Weekly* at a salary of twenty-seven dollars and fifty cents a week. This was around 1939 or 1940.

Rogers Terrill received a rather good salary. At least a hundred a week and possibly a hundred and twenty-five. His assistants got around forty a week.

Ken White, a full-fledged editor of *Dime Detective*, was paid fifty-five dollars a week. Edythe Seims was editor of the successful *G-8 and His Battle Aces*, and then took on *The Mysterious Wu Fang*. Her salary was fifty-five dollars a week. Before her marriage to Steve Fisher she employed a young assistant at twenty dollars a week.

I don't believe Harry Widmer at Magazine Publishers received more than fifty dollars a week. Among the highest paid pulp editors were the two lady editors, Fanny Ellsworth of *Ranch Romances* and Dorothy McIlwraith of *Short Stories*. I knew Dorothy's salary was one hundred dollars a week and I am sure Fanny Ellsworth got at least that much, possibly more.

I never knew what Joseph Shaw's salary was at *Black Mask*, but it was high, for the time. Possibly one hundred fifty dollars a week. It was a factor in his dismissal as editor in 1936 when the magazine's sales had fallen below the profit line.

A glass of beer in all of the Times Square pubs was

ten cents—a very large glass. And you got every fourth glass on the house. I sat one Sunday in the bar of the Forty-fourth Street Hotel and had thirteen glasses of beer. It didn't seem to bother me, but I finally got up to leave—and landed on the floor.

I am today virtually a teetotaler, but in those days I did a reasonable amount of social drinking. I seldom got into the intoxication stage, though. I was working too hard to do much drinking and I never did drink except at parties.

Chapter Twelve

In the spring of 1935 I made the rounds of Standard Magazines, Popular Magazines, Street & Smith and Magazine Publishers. I sold western stories to Standard Magazines, detective stories to Street & Smith, spy stories to Popular and both western and detective to Magazine Publishers.

I wrote a total of fifty-seven stories in 1935 and sold fifty-five of them. I had only two rejects (and have never had one since). Since my income for the year was around ten thousand dollars I must have written a considerable number of stories longer than five thousand words. And that was the goal, of course. The short stories went into the back of the magazines. The novelettes and "novels" were in front and the authors got their names on the covers. But you could sell only so many novelettes and I was continually trying to expand my markets.

It seemed the safest thing to do. A magazine could suddenly become overstocked and not buy from you for two or three months. It was best to spread out and have a larger number of markets. I made the rounds, to Dell (to whom I sold only one story in all the years I wrote for the pulps), all the way down to lower Broadway to Munsey. Munsey was considered a difficult market for beginning writers, but it was a substantial one and I hammered away at it.

The established companies were always starting new magazines. Some prospered, some did not and were quickly discontinued. Rogers Terrill started *Detective Tales* and I sold some stories to it. Edythe Seims was put in charge of *Wu Fang*, a pulp imitation of Dr. Fu Manchu. I sold her two stories and introduced her to Steve Fisher, who also sold her a couple of stories and began to woo her. They were married inside of three months.

Wu Fang did not go but the powers at Popular still thought the idea was good and later put Ken White in charge of a revised version, which bore the title *Dr. Yen Sin*. I sold two stories to this magazine also.

At Magazine Publishers they were always experimenting with new magazines. I sold stories to *Western Trails*, to *Ace Sports*, to *10 Detective Aces*, *Detective Romances* and others of the group.

I girded myself early in 1935 and called at the offices of Warner Publications, which published *Field and Stream*, *Ranch Romances* and the elite of all the pulps, *Black Mask*. I asked for no less a personage than Captain Joseph T. Shaw and wonder of wonders, he had me come into his office.

He was a charming man, extremely courteous and very much interested in young writers. He encouraged me to write a story for him. I did and he called me in and discussed it at great length, pointing out its shortcomings. I tried another story and another.

He was always genial, always friendly. He suggested revisions, discussing them in elaborate detail. He encouraged you to do revisions of revisions and when he finally rejected your story, it was always with great regret, a hand on your shoulder, a pat on the back. "Try again, old man. *Please!*"

Shaw wore me out with kindness, but I couldn't sell him a story. However, Fanny Ellsworth was across the hall and I was a western writer as well as a mystery man. Her *Ranch Romances* was one of the great successes of the pulp magazine business, possibly the most profitable of all pulp magazines. Fanny was perhaps thirty-two or thirty-three years of age at this time and had been the editor of the magazine for at least ten years.

She was an extremely erudite woman. You would have thought she would be more at home with a magazine like *Vogue* or *Harper's* than the guiding spirit of *Ranch Romances*. She knew what she wanted in her magazine, however, and had built up a solid group of writers, many of whom worked for her alone. The magazine came out twice a month and published a lead novel of twenty-five-thousand words, plus a novelette or two of ten thousand words and a number of short stories. The lead novels were written only by "name" writers and my ambitions were not yet that high. In fact, they were very low, having just been rejected across the hall.

I submitted a five-thousand-word short story to Fanny Ellsworth and she bought it at the base rate of one cent a word. I sold her two more in succeeding months.

Although I had campaigned unsuccessfully for the office of secretary of the American Fiction Guild shortly after my arrival in New York, I became, by a couple of quick events, the president of the New York chapter in the Spring of 1935. Arthur J. Burks, who had been one of the founders of the AFG was the national president in 1934. He decided to step aside and Norvell Page, then the president of the New York chapter, was elected national president. The secretary of the New York chapter moved up to president and I was appointed secretary of the New York chapter. Press of work caused the president of the New York chapter to resign and I moved up. I was shortly afterwards reelected president for a full term.

As president of the chapter it was my job to try to get out large attendances for the Friday luncheons and to do so it was necessary to get well-known speakers. I got some doozies. One, who drew a large crowd, was the Marquis de la Falaise, who had been married to Constance Bennett, the movie star.

Another was a character rather well known in New York circles, as he belonged to the Adventurers' Club and spoke at other groups. He claimed to be the greatest spy the world had ever known. He told of his adventures in the Boer War, when he had been a spy for the Boers. He had learned to hate all things British and in World War I he affirmed that he had been a spy for the Germans and was the man directly responsible for Lord Kitchener's death. He wrote an occasional article for a magazine, or Sunday supplement, along the same lines, but no one took him seriously.

This old windbag a spy? We joked about him. But the week following Pearl Harbor the FBI arrested some eighty members of a Nazi spy ring in New York. The leader was Fritz Duquesne, the old windbag.

He was a real spy, after all. Maybe he *had* been responsible for the death of Lord Kitchener!

It was about 1934 when Arthur J. Burks, who had been a Lieutenant in the Marines during World War I, began signing some of his adventure stories, *Lieutenant Arthur J. Burks*. It looked very good on a title page and soon a few "captains" began appearing in adventure magazines. Then majors and colonels. One writer finally topped them by signing his stories "General."

But Major was the popular rank. There were no less than a dozen majors on the contents pages of the adventure magazines. I remember one time at a bull session when a half dozen "Majors" were present the boys began nailing down one of them. In what branch of the service had he been commissioned? He was backed down on the American Army, transferred to the British, but a Britisher denounced him. He couldn't possibly have served in the British army and know so little about it.

The harried Major finally exclaimed that he had been a Major in the Australian Mounted Police and defied anyone to disprove it.

A writer spends so many hours inventing adventures for his fictional characters that he sometimes confuses fiction and fact. He begins to think that he himself has lived some of the adventures of which he has written.

Another pulp writer moved into the Forty-fourth Street Hotel, while I was living there. Several times a week he would knock on my door in the evening and come in and kick it around. Jack Reardon was often there and sometimes Mort Weisinger and Steve Fisher.

During one such session this writer began to relate some of his own adventures. He had been in the United States Marines for seven years, he had been an explorer on the upper Amazon for four years, he'd been a white hunter in Africa for three years. As he waxed enthusiastic about his exploits, I made a few notes, and after listening for a couple of hours, I said, "Ron, you're eighty-four years old, aren't you?"

He let out a yelp, "What the hell are you talking about? You know I'm only twenty-six."

I read from my notes. "Well, you were in the Marines seven years, you were a civil engineer for six years, you spent four years in Brazil, three in Africa, you barnstormed with your own flying circus for six years. . . . I've just added up all the years you did this and that and it comes to eighty-four years. . . ."

The writer blew his stack. I will say this, his extremely

vivid imagination earned him a fortune, some years later. He wrote one book that directly and indirectly earned him around a half million dollars in a single year.

One of the most active members of the American Fiction Guild and possibly the chief party-giver of the crowd was Harrison Forman. He claimed to be an authority on Tibet, having made several trips there. Since all writers of our group were suspect when they spoke of their adventures we took Forman's claims with a grain of salt, but not long afterwards he published a book *Through Forbidden Tibet*, and as a result became adviser on the motion picture, "Lost Horizons." Harrison was always going off on trips and I was astounded to hear him broadcasting from Danzig immediately after the outbreak of the war. Later I heard him broadcasting many times from Chung-king in China.

I have seen Harrison Forman a number of times through the years. He became one of the greatest travelers of all time and now and then he would stop off in Hollywood and have lunch or pay a visit. Through the years I have received postcards from him from Outer Mongolia, the Belgian Congo, from Timbuctoo, from Lake Titicaca.

Two or three years ago I was in the hospital having out the old gall bladder. I received a card from Forman from one of those exotic places and not having anything else to do, I began thinking about him. I began putting things together, recalling an incident that happened here, there, and I came to a conclusion that may or may not be right. I *think* it is right.

Since Harrison is at least five years older than I am, he has now retired from his travels, so it may be all right to reveal the conclusion that I came to about him. I think he had another job all through these years. His writing—which was only occasional—was the cover for his particular job which took him all over the world.

In the 1930's Harrison Forman was a dark, extremely handsome man. Had they been making the James Bond movies in those days he would have made an excellent James Bond.

A group of pulp writers made more noise than a gaggle of ten ganders and one goose and when they were drinking gin they made as much noise as two such gaggles.

The Depression days was the time of the Communist, we have learned since. But the majority of the pulp writers I knew in the 1930's were completely unpolitical. We were too busy trying to make a living to bother with politics. I recall that I was completely disinterested in the Civil War in Spain when it started in 1936.

I did not bother to register or vote in the 1936 political campaigns. I cared little for either Franklin D. Roosevelt or Alfred Landon. I thought Adolf Hitler was a German Charlie Chaplin. Huey Long was a clown.

Joe Stalin was none of my concern. Besides, wars were a thing of the past. Nobody in his right mind could ever think that there would ever be another war.

When I read a newspaper I turned first to the comic pages, then read some of the columnists. I seldom read the front pages. I did not even own a radio so never listened to the news broadcasts.

There were political arguments among the pulp writers now and then, but I never took part in any of them. I had no politics. And neither, I thought, did most of the pulp writers. But looking back now I am amazed at how naive some of us were.

Naturally, I knew about the political crisis in Europe, but I thought Hitler was bluffing. Nothing would ever come of it. Then Germany invaded Poland and I promptly bought a radio and began to stay up half the night listening to the news. I heard Hitler's voice on the radio and was shocked. This Charlie Chaplin type was a fantastic rabble-rouser. I began to understand how his screaming oratory had swayed his countrymen.

The war in Europe caused me to become politically conscious. Although I am of German descent, I was appalled by what Hitler had done and was doing. I learned that he had persecuted the Catholics even before he attacked the Jews and since I am a Roman Catholic, I automatically hated Hitler and all that he stood for.

In 1939 I was neither Democrat or Republican, but my father, back in Chicago, had been a Republican and when I voted the first time, shortly after attaining my majority, I voted Republican. Perhaps that as much as anything decided me to become a Republican. I rather liked Roosevelt's foreign policy, but when he ran for a third time and the Republicans put up Wendell Willkie I became a rabid Republican. Willkie was my type of politician. As was Tom Dewey who had been The Racket Buster in New York City, then District Attorney and was now governor of New York. I was later to meet Dewey and was completely unimpressed with him, but in 1940 I became an ardent supporter of Wendell Willkie.

This support of Willkie got me into a few arguments with some of the pulp writers and I began to understand, then, what had been behind some of the arguments I had been listening to for the past few years.

But Willkie was defeated and I went back to being nonpolitical. (Until I came to Hollywood.)

Chapter Thirteen

I coasted nicely through 1935 and into 1936. I was selling regularly to Street & Smith by now and was doing well with Standard Magazines, Popular and Magazine Publishers. I broke into *Detective Fiction Weekly*.

I had a few stories rejected by Duncan Norton-Taylor, the editor of DFW, but I promptly sold these to other magazines. Norton-Taylor was one of the handsomest young men I have ever known, and extremely erudite. He was marking time at *Detective Fiction Weekly*, preparing himself for more important things. He was soon to leave Munsey and go to work at *Time* magazine. He is today the head man on *Fortune* and I am not at all surprised.

I remember Duncan Norton-Taylor chiefly for a trivial incident. He bought a story from me for *Detective Fiction Weekly* and in view of the fact that I was now "in" he decided to take me to lunch. We were ready to leave when he peered out of the window and saw a slight mist coming down.

He promptly donned rubbers, raincoat and took

along a bumbershoot. I walked beside him on the street bareheaded, oblivious to the faint moisture while he plodded along with the umbrella over his head.

Duncan Norton-Taylor was soon followed by Charles Ingerman on *Detective Fiction Weekly*. Ingerman was cast from the same mold as Norton-Taylor. He was a philologist and could speak nine languages. When I first met him he was an assistant editor on *Operator #5*, but about 1936 he transferred over to Munsey's and by the law of succession became editor of *Detective Fiction Weekly*. He was as erudite as Norton-Taylor but lacked the latter's intensive will to succeed. I always had the feeling that Ingerman did not like the pulps, but when he was editor of DFW I sold him a number of stories.

I could not crack *Argosy*, the other big magazine at Munsey's. The magazine was a weekly and ran four serials simultaneously, a new one beginning every week. Ninety per cent of the serials were written by Max Brand, George Owen Baxter, George Challis, Evan Evans, and Fred MacIsaac.

It was a long time before I learned that the first four of these names were all pseudonyms of the legendary Frederick Faust.

Fred MacIsaac was a separate entity.

Chandler Whipple was for several years editor of *Argosy*. He was a reserved man, not too robust, save for a pair of huge mustaches. He did a little writing himself, selling a story now and then to Fanny Ellsworth of *Ranch Romances* and Art Lawson of Dell. I believe he published a couple of western books in later years, but they apparently were not too well received for he dropped from the writing ranks. I sold him but one story and that was in 1937.

Another editor who was indisposed toward me was Art Lawson. Unlike Whipple, who was reserved and soft-spoken, Lawson was brusque and outspoken and had a caustic tongue. I sold him only one story, also in 1937, but I dropped the Dell magazines from my route and never tried very hard there.

Lawson was also a writer, also selling an occasional story to *Ranch Romances*. He, too, fell along the literary wayside.

Harry Widmer began, I believe, as a writer and became an editor because he could not make a living as a writer. He was a pleasant, rather stout man and had the worst stammer of any person I have ever known. He would get stuck completely on a word and you would tense up and want to help him out, but then Harry would suddenly give it up and start all over.

Years later, Harry was an editor for a paperback company and I was astonished to learn that he had completely lost his stammer. And he was physically nicely streamlined.

Magazine Publishers had a bad habit of shaving all checks ten per cent. You got only forty-five dollars for a five thousand-word story, ninety dollars for a ten thousand-worder. Of course the smart writers marked their stories up. A five thousand-word story became a fifty-five hundred-worder, etc.

Now and then, however, they would take the time to

actually count the words in a story and mark you down. They did this to Roger Torrey once and he blew his stack.

Most of the editors were young. Leo Margulies was thirty-four in 1934, Rogers Terrill was thirty-five or six, Duncan Norton-Taylor was in his late twenties, as was Charlie Ingerman. Lawson and Whipple were in their early thirties.

John Nanovic was twenty-eight or nine, although already bald. He was only two or three years out of Notre Dame, not having entered college until the age of twenty-two or three. He was an earnest, sincere man, deeply religious (Roman Catholic) and the only editor I can recall who really liked the work he was doing. He liked the kind of stories he was using in *The Shadow, Doc Savage, Crime Busters*, etc. Once he began using an author regularly that author could do no wrong. He reported on all submissions in twenty-four hours and you got paid on Friday.

Only once after I had started selling Nanovic regularly did he reject a story of mine and I could have killed him afterwards. We were at a luncheon of the American Fiction Guild, John seated beside me, Leo Margulies across the table. John started kidding me about the story I had submitted to him earlier in the week, and the title, "Stamps of Doom"—wow!

Leo Margulies looked at me with a fishy eye, then turned to John. " 'Stamps of Doom,' eh? You think it's a *bad* story?"

"Dreadful," said John.

"Thanks," snarled Leo. "I just bought it today!"

One thing no author ever told an editor was that a story he was submitting had been rejected by another editor. The story was always hot off the typewriter, written expressly for this editor.

Leo Margulies was a short man, not over five feet five. He was a dynamic, forceful man with a low boiling point. I heard him laying out one of his assistants once, who was a full six feet five inches tall, calling him every name he could think of and some that he invented to give it more schmaltz. The big man took it all.

Several years later Leo took a course from Dale Carnegie and as a result his personality changed. He remained the aggressive business type, but his angry tirades became a thing of the past.

F. Orlin Tremaine of Street & Smith was editor of *Astounding Stories, Clues* and one or two other magazines. He was a week-day New Yorker, commuting every Friday to upper New York state where he owned a summer camp. F. Orlin (I never learned what the F stood for) saved every dollar he could and put it into the camp, which his wife and brother-in-law ran.

You won't believe F. Orlin's system of selecting stories for his magazine even if I tell you about it, but I'm going to tell it anyway.

All editors had a vast number of stories submitted to them, hundreds and hundreds every month. They came from literary agents by the dozen, they were delivered by the writers personally and they came in the mails, swarms of them.

The customary way was to read the stories by the KNOWN writers first, then have the assistants go through the "slush," all those stories by unknowns. The assistants would pass on the stories they liked to the editors, who would read them and make the final decision.

Not F. Orlin Tremaine. His assistants were merely copy editors. They read no stories. Tremaine read them all himself. "Names" meant nothing to him. He played no favorites. He wanted good stories only. He didn't care who wrote them.

So . . . as the stories came in Tremaine piled them up on a stack. All the stories intended for *Clues* in this pile, all those for *Astounding* in that stack.

Two days before press time of each magazine, Tremaine would start reading. He would start at the top of the pile and read stories until he had found enough to fill the issue. Now, to be perfectly fair, Tremaine would take the stack of remaining stories and turn it upside down, so next month he would start with the stories that had been on the bottom this month.

Nothing could be fairer than that.

Except . . .

What if the stack was five feet tall and Tremaine got all the stories he needed after reading only two feet of the stack? Next month he might also read only two feet of stories.

What if your story was in the middle of the pile—that foot of stories that did not get reached last month, this month, or . . . ?

Months would go by. The pleadings of agents and writers for a report on their stories, at least the return of the mss. went unheeded. Nothing could make Tremaine look through that stack of manuscripts.

I knew of writers whose stories were in the middle of a pile for over a year. One writer even claimed his story had been with Tremaine for over a year and a half.

In spite of Tremaine's system I sold him two or three stories, but these had gone to him only after they had been rejected elsewhere.

Chapter Fourteen

Early in 1936 I decided that since I was now well established with Standard Magazines I would try to come up with a series for them. I had Captain John Vedders going nicely in *Operator #5*, and I was also writing Douglas March regularly for *The Spider*.

I did not know it then but this decision was a milestone in my career.

For this series that I intended for *Thrilling Detective* I came up with Oliver Quade, the Human Encyclopedia. The first story I wrote featuring Quade was "Brass Knuckles" and Leo Marguiles and the boys in the back room all said that it was my best story. I wrote another, "Death at the Main" and followed with "Murder on the Midway," "Pictures of Death" and "Trailer Town." The magazine was overloaded and Leo told me to hold off writing further stories in the series until they could use some of them.

"Brass Knuckles" was not published until November, 1936, although I had written it in March.

I got a telephone call from the New York story editor

of Columbia Pictures, William C. Lengel, a former editor of *Cosmopolitan* and *Liberty*.

There was some interest in the story on the Coast. I was tremendously excited, for several chaps I had known had sold a story or two to motion pictures. Usually these were writers for *Black Mask*. Ted Tinsley had sold one for five hundred dollars and a couple of other chaps I knew had also received from two hundred fifty to five hundred dollars a story from the picture people.

Somehow, the thought of Hollywood had never occurred to me up to this time. Sure, I would have welcomed it, but Hollywood was very, very distant and those Hollywood sales, well, they were the *Black Mask* boys, of which I was not one. I was doing very well in the pulps, but I had given up the thought of cracking *Black Mask*. I had tried and had failed miserably.

Pictures?

I waited for Bill Lengel to call again. I even went in to see him. You never could tell about those boys on the Coast. They got interested, then lost interest.

In December "Death at the Main" was published in *Thrilling Detective*. I received another phone call from Lengel. The boys on the Coast were definitely interested. I had hardly hung up the phone than it rang again. Paramount Pictures. They were interested in The Human Encyclopedia. Within two days there were calls from David O. Selznick and Sam Goldwyn.

I had no agent. I knew nothing of pictures and picture people. I rushed down to Ed Bodin, asked him to help me. He went around and around and I went with him. Offers came through. Ed sifted them out and we decided upon David O. Selznick.

It called for a story sale and ten weeks' employment in Hollywood. Total, six thousand dollars.

I signed. I signed everything in sight without reading. What I actually signed was a thirty-day option which called for a payment of two hundred dollars for the option.

The option was not exercised. David O. Selznick had just bought a property called *Gone with the Wind*. He was no longer interested in a pulp magazine character called The Human Encyclopedia.

Columbia, Paramount and Goldwyn were no longer interested. If it wasn't good enough for David O. Selznick it wasn't good enough for them.

I had received a call from the Encyclopaedia Britannica Company. They loved The Human Encyclopedia character and were interested in sponsoring a radio series built around the character. They gave me gratis, free, a set of the *Encyclopaedia Britannica*. But when David O. Selznick failed to exercise the option the Britannica Company lost interest.

Six months later a radio show, "Information Please," went on the air.

A month ago I had not even thought of Hollywood. Now it was foremost in my thoughts. I could not work. What was the use of writing stories for fifty, sixty or even a hundred dollars when out there, in California, they were paying thousands and thousands of dollars?

I had not used an agent after those early few weeks in New York. Ed Bodin was a pulp agent. What I needed was a big time agent. I got one upon the recommendation of one of the people at the New York office of David O. Selznick.

He phoned me almost daily. He had a fifty thousand dollar deal with Samuel Goldwyn. The deal was off the next day, but he had a new one with Metro-Goldwyn-Mayer for seventy-five thousand dollars. Two days later the MGM deal had cooled, but Warner Brothers was offering one hundred thousand for The Human Encyclopedia.

I had a month of this. A month during which I did absolutely no writing. At the end of the month I fired this high-powered agent and faced the facts.

I was a pulp writer. I was getting a cent a word for my stories and I could make a very good living from it. All I had to do was work like hell. Perhaps I could become a good pulp writer and get my rates up to a cent and a half a word, perhaps—even two cents a word.

Chapter Fifteen

It is now 1937. I have not forgotten the near-success of The Human Encyclopedia, but I was back again pounding the typewriter day after day. I was uneasy, however. I was one of a hundred journeyman pulp writers, all receiving a cent a word. I was making a good living, my stories were selling but I was not progressing.

I had to do *something* to rise above the rank and file of pulp writers. After weeks of deliberation I came to a momentous decision. I would raise my rate of pay. Ninety per cent of my output was going to three houses, Popular, Standard and Magazine Publishers. I went around to them and announced that henceforth my rate was one and one-half cents a word.

The editors of all three of these houses promptly told me to go to hell. They added a few choice phrases, such as who the hell did I think I was? Etc. Etc.

I had gone out on the limb and the limb had been cut out from under me.

I had to go out and find new markets. Also, I had to nurse the couple I had left.

I made the long trip to Munsey's—it was 'way down at 280 Broadway in lower Manhattan, a long subway ride. I wrote what I considered an outstanding Western short story and gave it to the editor of *Argosy*, Chandler Whipple. He rejected it.

I knew that *Short Stories* was virtually a closed market, but I took the *Argosy* reject in to *Short Stories*. I met Dorothy McIlwraith for the first time. She was cool, formal, not too encouraging, as she had a stable of excellent, regular writers. I gave her one of my finest sales pitches, told her I had to have two cents a word, that the editors of *Argosy* and *Adventure* were laying siege to my door, but I liked *Short Stories* so much that I preferred to have my work appear in it.

I later became so well acquainted with Dorothy McIlwraith that we frequently discussed this first meeting of ours. I would guess that Dorothy was fifty-two or fifty-three years of age at this time. She was a native of Canada, who had been an editor for Doubleday for more than twenty years. A few years previously Doubleday had discontinued its chain of magazines. The bellwether of the string had been *Short Stories*, almost fifty years old. It was bought by William J. Delaney, an advertising salesman. He employed Dorothy to remain with the magazine she had already edited for years.

She was a heavyset woman who had never married. She lived in a small house on Long Island with another spinster.

She was an excellent editor.

The day after my all-out sales pitch, Dorothy telephoned me. She agreed with all that I had told her and was buying the story at MY PRICE OF TWO CENTS A WORD!

I promptly wrote a second story for Dorothy, which she also bought for two cents a word, then I plunged into the novelettes that dominated the magazine for the next several years. There was seldom an issue in the years to come that did not contain one of my long novelettes or serials.

The year before I had sold three short stories to Fanny Ellsworth of *Ranch Romances*. I now returned and told Fanny I would like to try a lead "novel" for her—for one and a half cents a word. Fanny hesitated and I gave her the Dorothy McIlwraith treatment. She consented finally to let me try a twenty-five thousand-worder.

I wrote "Wildcat Range" and she bought it for my new price. It was the first of many lead novels I wrote for the magazine. One of the very last stories I ever sold to a pulp was a serial for which Fanny paid me six cents a word!

When Joe Shaw was let go from *Black Mask* late in 1936, the owner, Eltinge Warner, gave the magazine to Fanny Ellsworth and a shock ran through the publishing world. A woman at the helm of *Black Mask?*

Fanny Ellsworth took it in stride. She had read some of my Human Encyclopedia stories in *Thrilling Detective*. With a little more polish she thought that they would do well in *Black Mask*.

"For two cents a word?" I asked.

"Two cents," said Fanny.

I wrote "Ask Me Another" in a lighter vein than I had written for *Thrilling Detective*. I added the character of Charlie Boston (under which name I later wrote the *Silver Jackass* for Reynal & Hitchcock). Fanny bought "Ask Me Another" and I was in *Black Mask*.

I wrote fourteen novelettes for *Black Mask* in the next three years. I saw my name on the cover over that of Carroll John Daly.

Christmas was approaching and I had had three stories published in *Black Mask*. I was invited to the *Black Mask* Christmas party which had become an institution. Writers came from all over the United States to attend this party. It was held in the offices of *Black Mask* and booze flowed freely.

I had helped Steve Fisher into *Black Mask* and we went to the party together. (He had helped me get into Street & Smith.) I cannot now remember who was at the party, but there was a contingent of writers from the West Coast and of course there were the *Black Mask* contributors from the East; Carroll John Daly, Roger Torrey, Lester Dent, Steve Fisher, James H. S. Moynahan, Nels Leroy Jorgenson, Baynard Kendrick and many others.

There were a few book editors present, prominent among them the editor of Crime Club. He was the one lad all the *Black Mask* writers catered to, for all wanted Crime Club to publish their books.

A crap game started and in a crap game I take a back seat to no one. I learned about crap shooting in the

Army when I was only sixteen. I perfected my skill in the alleys of Chicago.

The Crime Club editor was throwing his weight around. (Or maybe it was the booze.) I had the dice and he yelled "cocked dice" and started to pick up the money.

I said, "Put it down."

Crime Club looked me squarely in the eye. Steve said: "Put it down or Frank'll punch you in the nose."

I said, "Steve said it."

The Crime Club editor put down the money, quit the game and left the party. I was dead at Crime Club.

Cornell Woolrich was not at the *Black Mask* party, but he was one of the leading contributors to the magazine, as well as other leading pulps of the time. Woolrich was an introvert who lived with his mother at the Hotel Marseilles on upper Broadway and left the hotel only when absolutely necessary. He shunned parties and social gatherings, but Steve Fisher and I got him out to a party one night. The next day I got a call from Fanny Ellsworth. "What did you fellows do to Cornell Woolrich last night?" she asked.

"Nothing," I replied. "We got him to take a couple of drinks, that's all."

Fanny went on: "He came tearing in here this morning yelling that I was paying Gruber, Fisher and Torrey four cents a word and he was getting only one and a half cents and he was never going to write for the magazine again!"

I didn't recall that we had told Woolrich that little

fib about our word rates, but we *could* have done so.

Later, when I was well established at Rinehart, the company brought out a book by Cornell Woolrich and I asked Stanley Rinehart what he thought of him. Stanley said that he had never met him, all the negotiations had been done by mail—although Woolrich lived in New York City!

Another time Steve and I were in Yorkville with our wives, having a few beers, and we decided to phone Woolrich and ask him to join us. His mother answered the phone and gave us holy hell—and refused to put him on the phone.

Carroll John Daly was a rather slight man, possibly five feet eight or nine inches tall. Although he did not resemble his famous character, Race Williams, physically, he liked to talk like him and once Carroll—who was not much of a drinker ordinarily—got tanked and was arrested on the way back to White Plains. He was carrying a .45, which did not set well with the police, for the carrying of concealed weapons in New York State is one of the most heinous of all felonies.

Daly needed dental work very badly, but had a phobia about dentists and would not go to have the work done. His wife was continually after him about it.

I enjoyed our bridge sessions tremendously, for Daly was my type of bridge player. He refused to take the game seriously and when we teamed up as partners against opponents who did not know us well, we would drive them crazy. I recall one indignant lady who got up and quit the game when he bid "six no spades."

101

One of the most regular contributors to *Black Mask*, Roger Torrey, was extremely fond of the sauce. I once ran into him on Madison Avenue at nine o'clock in the morning. He was either still loaded from the night before or had gotten an early start that morning.

Personally, Roger Torrey was a tough little guy, as hard as the characters he portrayed so well in his stories.

Speaking of drinking, Steve gave a party one night; I think it was a New Year's party and he invited about fifty or sixty of the hardy ones to the party. I still remember vividly the scene when Otis Adelbert Kline, the science fiction writer, who had brought his mandolin with him, kept leaning his two hundred and fifty pounds against the very thin and slight Lurton Blassingame, and Blassingame, who enjoyed the nickname "Count" because of his dignified appearance and sober mien, kept trying to get away from Kline. I finally rescued him, then Otis started leaning against me.

Speaking of parties—in my very early days in New York, George Bruce, who had a temporary apartment in Brooklyn, gave one. It was a rather small apartment and the thirty-some guests who were there were jammed into the place so that you could hardly move around. About ten o'clock in the evening George announced that he had a deadline for a twelve thousand-word story the following morning and had to get at it. I assumed that it was a hint for the guests to leave, but such was not the case at all. George merely went to his desk in one corner of the room and began to bang his electric typewriter. George sat at that typewriter for four solid hours, completely oblivious to the brawl going on around him. At two o'clock in the morning he finished his twelve thousand words and had a drink of gin.

They don't make them like that any more!

In the 1920's, when I became a reader of the pulps and long before I sold my first story, my favorites were H. Bedford Jones and Fred MacIsaac. I did not meet Jones until I was one of the leading contritutors to *Short Stories* magazine. I was still in awe of his reputation, but it turned out that Jones was more interested in my own tremendous production at the time.

I did not see him again until years later, when he had virtually quit writing. It was in the shop of a rare book dealer in Beverly Hills. I scarcely noticed the elderly man sitting quietly in a corner, who got into a conversation with my six-year-old son, Bob (who is now twenty-seven). The shop owner finally said, "I'd like you to meet a real old-timer, Henry Jones." I looked at the elderly man and Jones got up and said very quietly, "Hello, Frank, we met some years ago in New York . . ."

It was H. Bedford Jones.

I must report one other incident which causes me to wince a little to this day. How could we ever have been so brash in those days?

The great Fred MacIsaac attended one of our luncheons in early 1938. I got to talking with him and he invited me to come down to his hotel later in the afternoon to have a drink.

Publishers always paid on Fridays and it was our

custom to go around Friday afternoons and pick up our checks. I picked up a couple of good ones at *Ranch Romances* and *Black Mask,* and a couple more at Street & Smith. The checks totaled over eight hundred dollars.

I went down to the Hotel Chelsea on Twenty-Third Street, where MacIsaac was staying. We chatted for awhile and he asked how I was doing. I could not resist trying to impress MacIsaac, one of the real giants of the business, so pulled out the checks and showed them to him.

"This week's," I said with restrained modesty. He looked at the checks and commented: "I wouldn't mind having a couple of those myself." I thought he was being indulgent with me and thought no more of it at the time . . . but six weeks later MacIsaac shot himself through the head and the story came out. He had not sold a story in more than six months and had not saved any of the huge sums he had earned through the years.

That same afternoon with MacIsaac he took me up the street to a cafe where the great Thomas Wolfe did most of his writing. He, too, was living at the Chelsea Hotel and MacIsaac knew him well. He introduced me to Wolfe and we sat at the table and listened to a three-hour monologue by Wolfe. The subject was how great a writer he was.

I did not like Thomas Wolfe and I still think fondly of Fred MacIsaac who had a million readers for every thousand who preferred Wolfe.

Chapter Sixteen

I have always been intrigued by the vocations of writers or jobs that writers were engaged in before taking up the craft of writing. Offhand, I cannot recall more than two writers who studied journalism or writing in college. In fact, very few of the writers I knew actually went to college.

Walter Gibson was a magician, an assistant to the fabulous Harry Houdini. After Houdini's death Walter worked with The Great Thurston. He wrote a book revealing the escape methods of Houdini and this led him into writing. Soon he was tapped to do *The Shadow*. He never lost his interest in magic and after writing *The Shadow* for sixteen years he went back into magic, traveling with the late Harry Blackstone.

He was always a very nervous chain-smoker, lighting a fresh cigarette from the butt of another. The night before our son, Bob, was born, Walter came out to visit us in Scarsdale. He was living at the time in a hotel on Twenty-Fourth Street. In order to get to our place he had to take the subway to Times Square, the Shuttle to

Grand Central, then the train to Scarsdale. In Scarsdale he had to get to our apartment via taxicab. Since he arrived at our place around seven, he traveled all the way, during the evening rush and anyone who knows New York knows how the passengers are packed into the subways and interurban trains.

Shortly after his arrival he performed a new magic trick he had just learned. The climax was changing a roll of toilet tissue into an egg, which he broke into a glass. In order to do the trick he had to bring his "tools" with him and I still chuckle thinking about Walter bringing that tissue and egg concealed on his person during the long trek to our place. Walter's pockets were always bulging with magic paraphernalia. I once kidded him into emptying his pockets and among other items he produced eight packs of playing cards.

Lester Dent was also somewhat of a magician as was Ken Crossen who succeeded to the editorship of *Detective Fiction Weekly* in the late thirties. Clayton Rawson, who wrote mystery novels and is today managing editor of *Ellery Queen's Mystery Magazine*, was a good enough magician to become a professional.

Lester Dent was born in Oklahoma and used to joke about never having worn shoes until he became eighteen. He was a telegraph operator for years until he hit as a writer.

The most unusual occupation of any writer I have ever known was that of Borden Chase, who became very big in *Detective Fiction Weekly* and *Argosy* before coming to Hollywood. Borden was a sandhog for a time, but gave that up when he took a job as "secretary" for a notorious gangster—one of the really top bullet-and-gun boys.

That word "secretary" should be studied carefully. In this job Borden had a lot of time while his employer was in conferences with business associates, and Borden used to kill time by reading detective and gangster magazines. One day it occurred to him that he could write better stories than those he read and he began to do so. He caught on very quickly for his stories carried a ring of authority.

Borden's real name was Frank Fowler. He acquired the pseudonym, he told me, during a short walk from the subway to the offices of the Munsey Company, when he passed a Borden Milk Company Truck standing in front of the Chase National Bank.

When I first met Borden he was still working as a "secretary," but he soon resigned to devote his full time to writing.

I must add that I asked Borden recently if he minded if I revealed his background and he chuckled and said, "What the hell, go ahead, a great many people already know it."

Borden came to Hollywood in the late 1930's and was soon knocking them dead. I don't know how often he got single checks of between fifty thousand dollars and one hundred thousand dollars for screenplays for John Wayne and other top stars.

For years, during the 1950's, Borden had the most fantastic writing contract at Universal that any writer ever had. His salary was around four thousand dollars a week, payable fifty-two weeks of the year, but he had to work only thirty-five weeks. He could write anything else he wanted on the side during the seventeen-week layoff.

Norvell Page was that rarity, a newspaper man turned fiction writer. He worked on the *New York World-Telegram* as a rewrite man for several years, although he was originally from either South or North Carolina.

I don't know what happened to Norvell Page. I heard that he had Ted Tinsley quit writing during the war and went to work for the government, but I have not heard of either in many years.

Alan Hathway who wrote a number of stories for John Nanovic of Street & Smith, was a reporter for the *New York Daily News*. He dropped out of writing and is today the managing editor of the extremely successful *Newsday* on Long Island.

Ned O'Doherty who also wrote much for John Nanovic, was a customs inspector at the New York Port.

Steve Fisher's only job before turning writer was that of a sailor in the United States Navy.

The only job Arthur J. Burks ever held down was that of a Marine. He had become a second Lieutenant in World War I and stayed on in the service. He was in Haiti or Nicaragua when he began writing. He resigned from the Marines in either 1926 or 1927 and came to New York. He reentered the Marines in World War II and rose to be a Colonel.

Theodore Tinsley, the *Black Mask* writer, worked for years in the office of a large insurance company. George

MacDonald, who wrote many lead novels for *The Phantom*, was for years the advertising manager of a large carpet company.

Erle Stanley Gardner, as everyone knows, was an attorney in Ventura and Oxnard, California. He had many Chinese clients and got to know the Chinese people very well, which knowledge he used so well in his Ed Jenkins stories for *Black Mask*.

I must tell you this. Today's big authority on Flying Saucers and UFOs was for years a pulp writer. He wrote for *G-8* and *His Battle Aces*, edited by Edythe Seims, who became Steve Fisher's wife.

Here is the plot of the only story I ever read in *G-8* which I believe was written by Donald E. Keyhoe. If not, it was by another writer, and I apologize.

"The Red Baron" was decimating the A.A.F. Planes crashed and the pilots were found horribly mutilated, ripped to shreds, etc. The payoff: The Red Baron had trained a tiger which he took along on his plane. He got over the poor American plane and the tiger jumped from The Baron's plane into the luckless Americans'. He had his lunch from the American pilot, then the Red Baron got underneath the American plane and the tiger jumped back into the Red Baron's plane.

Anyone for Flying Saucers?

Dashiell Hammett was a detective for the Pinkerton Detective Agency. The Continental Op and the agency he worked for are from Hammett's own background.

Nels Leroy Jorgenson was a motorcycle policeman in New Jersey all through the years he wrote for *Black*

Mask. He might have been the very tall, fierce-looking cop who gave you a ticket on the New Jersey turnpike.

Cornell Woolrich was still a student at college when he won the ten thousand dollars literary prize that *College Humor* gave in the early 1930's. The editor of the magazine at that time, and for many years, was the H. N. Swanson who became the top Hollywood literary agent.

Richard Sale dropped out of Washington and Lee College while either a junior or senior to write for the pulps, which he had already begun to crack.

Carroll John Daly was first an usher, then an assistant manager in a motion picture theatre. I don't think he ever became a manager. He tried acting, but did not like it, and his uncle, a very famous attorney, financed him to take a fling at writing.

One of the most hilarious evenings I ever enjoyed was listening to Daly tell about his experiences as a "receiver" for a bankrupt trunk company. His uncle, very influential in New York politics, got Daly this political plum—and that's what "receiverships" were in the Tammany Hall days. It was fortunate for the New York Bankruptcy courts that Carroll John Daly began selling his stories during his brief tenure as a receiver.

Joe Archibald, who wrote much for Standard and Magazine Publishers, was originally a cartoonist. He ruined many a tablecloth at the American Fiction Guild luncheons. The waiters did not appreciate the cartoons he drew on the cloths.

Ryerson Johnson was a coal miner in Southern Illinois before he attended the University of Illinois, where he studied journalism under William Byron Mowery, who himself became a very successful pulp writer. One of Johnny's classmates was George Armin Shaftel who became an excellent western story writer. George was very good as a rope twirler. Ryerson Johnson, incidentally, was very good with a musical saw. He tramped through Europe one year and saved a man's life in Bulgaria which led to his being asked to perform with the saw in the Bulgarian National Opera.

Ernest Haycox told me that he supported himself while attending the University of Oregon by working as news butcher on a train during summer vacations.

Chapter Seventeen

It is my intention to keep this narrative to the New York days, which began in 1934 when I arrived there and ended in 1943, when I left to come to Hollywood, but I have made several mentions of the "legendary" Max Brand and I am going to skip ahead, at this point, and talk about him.

Yes, I finally met Max Brand.

In 1943 I was working at Warner Brothers Studios and one day noted a new name on the directory in the Writers' Building. *Faust, F.* It dawned on me that this might be the legendary one himself, as I had heard that he had returned to America on the eve of the war in Europe and was supposed to be in Hollywood.

I went to his office, which was only a short distance up the hall from my own.

Yes, he admitted that he sometimes wrote under the name Max Brand. He was shy, somewhat aloof, I thought, but after I told him that I had sold a few hundred stories to the pulps he warmed up a bit. It was not an easy conversation but before I left he expressed the desire to read something I had written. I gave him two books.

A few days later he came into my office and began talking about one of the books. He went on about it for half an hour, discussing the book, *Simon Lash: Private Detective*. He was very warm in his evaluation of one of the minor characters, Jeff Spotted Tail, and suggested that I write a book with Jeff Spotted Tail as the chief protagonist.

He later read the other book I had given him but from his reticence to talk about it I judged that he did not think highly of it. Heinie was that way. He never criticized anyone (with the exception of Hollywood producers, which is normal for any writer). If he liked something he spoke profusely about it; if he didn't, he said nothing.

It was on the second visit with Faust that he insisted I call him Heinie and I learned later that it was the only name any of his friends called him. Max Brand, the name under which he is best known, was to him merely a literary pseudonym; he thought no more of it than he did of the other fourteen names under which he had written. In person, Heinie was the most fantastic, the most fabulous, the most vivid personality I have ever known.

He was a hard man to get to know, but once you got acquainted with him he held nothing back. He gave you his full friendship. And a very worthwhile friend Heinie was.

I can still see him squinting at me with the right eye

almost closed, the sly grin on his face. I can still hear that beautiful, melodious voice as he spoke with the utmost fluency, the most perfect diction.

Steve Fisher came to work at Warners a few weeks later. I introduced him to Heinie Faust and for the next year the three of us had a bull session just about every working day. Steve was as fascinated with Heinie as I was.

Heinie did all of his writing in the morning. He came to work at nine-thirty, sat down on a sofa in his office and with a typewriter on a straight-backed kitchen chair in front of him typed out fourteen pages. Fourteen pages each and every day.

No more, no less.

I grew up on the stories of Max Brand. By the time I met him I knew that he was probably the most prolific author of all time, although his writing life, save for motion pictures, was already behind him. When he came to Hollywood he practically ceased writing magazine or book fiction.

I asked him one time about the forty-five million words he was reputed to have written in his lifetime. He admitted that the figure was probably right. He wrote approximately one and a half million words a year for thirty years. When I asked him how he managed this terrific production, he answered with a question: "Can you write fourteen pages in one day?"

I replied that I had frequently written much more than that in a day. Unfortunately, I also went two or three weeks without writing a line. That, declared Heinie, was the trick. You had to write fourteen pages each and every day of the year. It added up to a million and a half words a year.

Heinie had trained himself to do it. Fourteen pages a day, come rain, come shine, come mood or no, Heinie wrote the fourteen pages.

He wrote them in two hours every morning.

Heinie was the most prolific writer of all time.

He was also the biggest boozer I have ever known.

That is, I realize, a shocking, apparently callous statement to make about a man of whom you have such fond memories, whom you admired so greatly. Yet to talk about Heinie Faust without referring to his drinking is impossible. Drinking was so great a part of his life, so vitally important to him. It affected his character, his work, everything about Heinie, that it simply cannot be ignored.

No man is perfect. You love your friends for their good qualities. You ignore their weaknesses. Heinie was a very human man. He had strong likes, he had prejudices.

Although I am today practically a teetotaler, I have done my share of drinking and I come from a drinking family. In view of this, I repeat: Heinie Faust was the greatest drinker I have ever known. He came to work in the morning carrying a quart thermos bottle full of whiskey. By noon this was gone. His lunch consisted of twelve to fifteen drinks. During the afternoon he dashed out through the back gate about once an hour and had three quick rum drinks in a handy bar. When he went

home at five-thirty he had a light supper and then settled down to his serious drinking.

The amount of whiskey Heinie Faust put away in the
course of a day was enormous.

He was no secret drinker. He spoke of it quite freely.
He was a big man physically, six feet three inches tall
and weighing close to two hundred pounds. There
wasn't an ounce of fat on his body. His hands were
enormous.

It was not until late afternoon that his drinking
began to take effect and even then it was not discernible
to the average person. Heinie never became a maudlin
drunk, he never passed out and he was certainly not a
slobbering drunk. After putting away close to two quarts
of whiskey during an eight-hour day, Heinie appeared to
the casual observer to be merely an aloof, perhaps ab-
sent minded person.

We often spoke of Heinie's drinking. He said
simply that he could not write until he had taken a few
drinks and "gotten away from the world." He required
an alcoholic stimulant to transport him into that world
of fantasy of which he wrote so well.

Heinie's was a strong personality. He had the utmost
confidence in himself, was extremely forceful and articu-
late. He had a vast contempt for all of Hollywood and
especially for the type of writing that is necessary for the
screen. Heinie was not a success in Hollywood. Hollywood never understood him and no one was able to tap
his extremely great talent.

Heinie was a writer of "originals." He never mastered

116

the technique of adapting an original into screenplay form. He made no effort to learn. He said screenplay writing was an artificial form of writing and would have none of it. After creating the Dr. Kildare series with which MGM made millions the studio let him go. He went to Columbia where he was also dropped after contributing one "original" story. He next came to Warners where he remained a year. No screenplay he wrote at Warners reached the screen. Heinie's name was often on the screen, but only as the author of the original story, never as having written the screenplay.

Heinie's first assignment at Warners was for Hal Wallis. He wrote the screenplay for a novel the studio had bought, *The Conspirators*. It was a dreadful screenplay and Heinie was taken off it.

At this particular time I was very hot at Warners. I had gone to work for the studio in December on a story called "Three Strangers." After his smashing success with *The Maltese Falcon*, John Houston had written an original story of some twenty pages. He had sold it to the studio for ten thousand dollars and was assigned, at two thousand dollars a week, to write the screenplay. He went off to the war and Henry Blanke, the producer, did not like Houston's screenplay. I was hired to rewrite it, or rather to start from scratch using only the basic idea from Houston's original.

Blanke was the producer of "The Maltese Falcon" and I always considered him the best producer I ever worked for in Hollywood.

I completed the assignment. Blanke liked it tremendously but could not cast it and the script was put on the shelf. I was given a contract by the studio and assigned to a story that was eventually called "Northern Pursuit." It starred Errol Flynn. On this script I followed William Faulkner, which is a story by itself. Jack Chertok was the producer of "Northern Pursuit." After completing the assignment I went back to Henry Blanke and he put me on Eric Ambler's novel, A *Coffin* for *Dimitrios*. I got a solo credit on this screenplay.

I had been at the studio only six months, but had written three screenplays, so when Heinie Faust was taken off "The Conspirators," Hal Wallis asked for me. I was working on it during the first few weeks of my acquaintanceship with Heinie.

An item came out in the papers that Hal Willis was going to cast Greta Garbo in the woman's role. Heinie read it and came storming into my office.

"This changes the whole picture," he exulted, "If I had known Garbo was going to play the part I would have written it entirely different. Frank, this is wonderful . . . I want to work with you on this screenplay. We will make it a great picture. I am going right over to Hal Wallis' office and ask to be put back on the script *with* you."

I tried to demur. In a collaboration there must be one boss, one man who makes the final decisions. Heinie's personality was much too strong. I could not work with him as much as I liked and respected him. I tried to tell this to Heinie but he refused to listen.

He went off to see Hal Wallis.

118

I picked up the phone, called Wallis and told him Heinie was on his way over to see him. I told him how I felt, but the decision was up to him. If he wanted to, he could put him back on the script, but in that case I would go off it.

Ten minutes later Heinie came back to my office. He opened the door, stood in the doorway and with his right eye almost closed and that sly grin on his face, he said: "You bastard!"

He left and I spent a very bad afternoon and evening. But the next morning Heinie came storming into my office, shook hands, said he'd had time to think about it and I was absolutely right.

We became closer friends than ever.

Incidentally, I flopped on this assignment. Wallis liked to have two or three writers working simultaneously on a script, with none of the writers knowing others were working on it. (This is now against the Writers' Guild rules.) He would take one scene from one writer, another from the second, one from the third and patch them together.

I learned that Lillian Hellman was working ahead of me, in New York, that there was another writer at the studio working behind me and I lost interest in the script and finally asked to be taken off it.

When the script was completed I was still entitled to a partial screen credit but I didn't like the script and waived the credit.

Greta Garbo did not play the woman's part. Hedy Lamarr did, with Paul Henreid as the leading man.

Once I asked Heinie who, in his opinion, was the best pulp editor he had ever written for. Without hesitation he replied, "Howard Bloomfield."

I was jolted, for this was also my own opinion.

I shouldn't relate the next incident, but what the hell. We used to pitch quarters against the wall. That is, we lagged quarters, but the toss was for a dollar a crack. We did this about three days a week for months, and Heinie lost twenty dollars every time. He always stopped when he had lost the twenty.

The average man has one of three vices, he drinks, he gambles or he chases women. Some have all three and that is bad, but I had only one vice—gambling. I was a terrific gambler for most of my life (although I am now reformed), but during the war I was the gin rummy champion of Warners and you have heard me make other references to gambling. There is a trick to everything and if you are good at gambling in one game, you quickly learn the tricks of another. The trick in pitching quarters is getting down low and throwing the coin so that it will land and slide the last few inches.

I got so I could touch the wall with the quarter nine times out of ten. This soon became evident in our quarter pitching. Heinie stood straight and tall and threw the quarter. The coin frequently hit the wall and bounced back.

Steve and I became conscience stricken after winning the twenty from him a number of times. We tried to quit the quarter pitching, but Heinie would insist on playing. He would become indignant when we tried to stall out of it.

He lost several hundred dollars pitching quarters over a period of time. It was years before I understood Heinie's reason for wanting to waste time at such a frivolous thing. He had such a contempt for Hollywood that it amused him to think of what it cost the studio for three contract writers to spend a half hour or an hour pitching quarters. It was worth twenty dollars to Heinie.

During the year of our almost daily talks, we discussed writing a great deal. We talked of Heinie Faust very little. Heinie liked to talk about you, your writing, your problem. Yet in the course of this year I did elicit certain things from him. He told me that he had originally wanted to be a poet, but living in New York in 1917 he had a roommate who was trying to write popular fiction. Pressed for money, Heinie decided to take a shot at a story himself.

He wrote a short story and sent it to Bob Davis at Munsey's. Davis promptly bought the story. Heinie wrote a second story which was also bought and he received with the check a summons to the august presence of Bob Davis.

Davis told Heinie of the immense popularity at this time of Zane Grey. He suggested that the western field offered great possibilities for another writer. He believed that Heinie could be a second Zane Grey. He thought that Faust should adopt a pseudonym, a short, easy to remember name with perhaps a western flavor. Thus "Max Brand" came into existence.

Davis ordered a serial from the twenty-five-year-old Faust, who had thus far written only two short stories. Heinie went to his room, wrote a serial in a very few days and was launched on his long, fabulous writing career.

During the years of his greatest popularity, from 1926 to 1938, Heinie lived in Italy. He referred to his home near Florence as a house or villa, but I have seen pictures of it and castle would be a better description. It was here that Heinie, whose great love was poetry, whose hobby was the study of the Renaissance Period, wrote his many, many western stories.

For years Max Brand was the undisputed "King of the Pulps." He received as high as ten cents a word during the golden decade of the 1920's. Even during the Depression years his rate never went below five cents a word. It was not until the middle thirties that he found it difficult to maintain a five-cent-a-word rate and this, along with the gathering war clouds in Europe, prompted him to forsake his beloved Italy and return to the United States. He lived in New York for a few months, turning out some smooth paper stories, but found the atmosphere not to his liking. A Dr. Kildare story sold to the movies and he came to Hollywood. He launched himself on this new career, was soon earning fifteen hundred dollars a week and virtually ceased writing for the magazines.

The closing chapters of Heinie's life are difficult to write. Neither Steve Fisher nor myself have ever gotten over a feeling of guilt for having somehow had a part in Faust's tragic end.

In early 1944 Steve was working at Warners on a war story. A Colonel Nee was sent out from Washington as a technical adviser. He sat in on our bull sessions in the late afternoons. I call attention to the phrase "in the late afternoons," for by then Heinie had imbibed his two quarts of whiskey. Of course we talked about the war; it was the number one subject of conversation and Heinie would say to Colonel Nee: "What I would like to do is get assigned to a company of foot soldiers, live with them, talk with them and write about them." Colonel Nee would say: "I can fix it for you," and either Steve or I would add, "Yeah, Heinie, why don't you do that? You could write a great war novel."

We were just making talk. I was forty years old in 1944, not likely to be drafted, and Steve had varicose veins. So we encouraged Heinie and he talked about his novel. The next morning, cold sober, he would come in and shudder.

"What the hell was that nonsense we were talking about yesterday? Me go over to Italy? I'm fifty-two years old, I've got no business in a shooting war."

But late that afternoon he would again talk about getting an assignment to go to Italy and again Colonel Nee would say: "I can fix it for you."

Weeks went by. Steve's war picture was shelved and Colonel Nee returned to Washington. But a few weeks later Heinie came into my office white-faced. "Look," he said, thrusting a letter at me, "Colonel Nee has fixed it. He's gotten me an assignment from *Harper's Magazine* as a war correspondent and I can leave for Italy next week."

Both Steve and I were shocked. Talking was one

thing. We had never really expected Heinie would go. We now tried to talk him out of it. Heinie said he would have no part of it. In the morning. In the afternoon he would again play with the idea.

Several more weeks went by. Heinie came in one day and said, "It's all settled. I'm going to Italy."

Six weeks later he was dead.

Chapter Eighteen

As I write this in January, 1967, the legend of *Black Mask* and The *Black Mask* School of Writing has reached full fruition. That *Black Mask* was a prestige magazine of mystery stories was only too well known during the 1930's. That the magazine and its style of writing would become legendary was, however, inconceivable, even in its heyday, and especially to the writers who were appearing in the magazine or hoped to enter its distinguished portals.

I did not myself become a reader of the magazine until around 1931 and 1932, but by the time I reached New York I was well aware of its position and in my early contacts with other writers and editors I heard much, much talk about *Black Mask*. It was *the* mystery magazine and Captain Joseph T. Shaw was *the* editor. Its contributors were the envy of all the other writers.

I accepted all of this. I accepted all the gossip and talk about *Black Mask*. I accepted that Captain Joseph Shaw had been an officer in World War I, that he was a master fencer and had invented a parry or thrust with the épée for which there was no defense.

I was a tremendous fan of the magazine and I had an admiration for all of its writers. I don't recall that I was especially envious of them, but I did hope one day to join their select group.

One by one I began to meet the *Black Mask* writers. Lester Dent and Theodore Tinsley were the first, I believe, but I soon met Roger Torrey, James H. S. Moynahan, Nels Leroy Jorgenson, Cornell Woolrich, Carroll John Daly, Frederick Nebel, George Harmon Coxe and the others who lived in and around New York. On my first trip to the West a few years later I met W. T. Ballard, H. Randolph Peacock, Norbert Davis, John K. Butler and Erle Stanley Gardner.

I have heard talk of *Black Mask* for more than three decades. It was bull session talk, shop talk. I have listened to a thousand hours of talk about the *Black Mask* school of writing. I have myself talked about it for some hundreds of hours. I have had a hundred different people tell me the history of *Black Mask*. And a number of these people were involved in its history, helped to make it. I was a part of it myself.

So, let's take a close, hard look at the history of the magazine. We'll begin by throwing aside all of the "talk" that there has been on this subject. Including some I have said myself, or in my writings.

I do not know if there is a complete set of *Black Mask* in the hands of any collector or university library. The University of California at Los Angeles has as complete a set as I have seen, yet they lack many of the early numbers. To collect a complete set is possible, but it would be a time-consuming, expensive job. UCLA has not been able to do it. Mr. Wilbur Smith, head of the Special Collections at UCLA and in charge of the copies of *Black Mask* would like very much to complete the university's collection. As I am sure would Professor Philip Durham of UCLA, who uses *Black Mask* and its school of writing in his English classes.

I have studied the file copies in the Special Collections at UCLA. They do not have Volume 1, Number 1, but they do have a very brittle, faded copy of Volume 1, Number 2, the second issue of the magazine. It is dated May, 1920, which indicates that the first edition of the magazine was dated April, 1920.

The owner of the magazine is given as Pro-Distributors' Publishing Company, the corporation that owned the magazine for twenty years, until it was sold to Popular Publications in the early 1940's.

The president of the company is listed as A. W. Sutton. Vice-president and Circulation Director is P. C. Cody, who was apparently with the company from the very beginning and of whom more anon.

I had always heard that the company had been owned by Eltinge Warner, from the very beginning, so in this matter already I concede I am wrong.

The editor of this second issue is given as F. M. Osborne, whose name I have never heard before. It was completely unknown during my years in New York. I have heard no one mention the name, not even Carroll John Daly.

This Number 2 issue of *Black Mask* seems to have

been confined to short stories entirely, for the list of contributors is large. They are:

Hamilton Craigie

J. J. Pearce, Jr., and Joseph Faus

Harold Ward

Ashton Crowell

Hamilton Craigie and Walter Grahame

Valentine Williams

Schuyler Hamilton

Maurice Leval

Greye La Spina

Frank Leighton

Hamilton Craigie and Walter Grahame

C. S. Montanye

Merlin Moore Taylor

Clinton Harcourt

Hamilton Craigie had three contributions in this one issue, one solo and two in collaboration.

Try this list of mystery writers on any current mystery fan. See how many names, if any, he can identify. The only names that stir a faint memory in my own mind are those of Valentine Williams and C. S. Montanye. Montanye was still writing for the pulps when I arrived on the scene in 1934, and I believe I have seen Valentine Williams' name on some old mystery novels published in the first decade or two of the twentieth century.

The UCLA library also has a copy of Volume 2, Number 2 dated December, 1920. Apparently there were six issues to a volume, but this was actually the eighth issue of *Black Mask*. F. M. Osborne is still listed as the editor and the contributors were:

Ralph Cummins
J. B. Hawley
H. de T. Roussel
Harold Ward
Lewis H. Moreton
Wilson Clay Missimer
L. H. Kilpatrick
Frederick Bruegger
Frederick Ames Coates
Paul Everman
Julian Kilman

Try *those* names on your modern mystery fan!

In Volume 2, Number 6, March, 1921, the twelfth issue of *Black Mask*, we finally come upon a name that not only rings a bell but tolls it good and loud. Vincent Starrett, the dean of American literary critics, who still holds forth in Chicago, is a contributor.

F. M. Osborne is still the editor.

Comes now a gap in the UCLA collection, but *Black Mask* has apparently become successful and has gone from a monthly to twice a month. This apparently occurred during 1922, but since I have been unable to find any 1922 copies I cannot give the exact date.

We pick up the chronology again with the March 15, 1923, issue. F. M. Osborne is still the editor. The magazine has changed its policy, somewhat. It contains installments of two serials, one by Frances James, titled "Sinister Images," and the second by Eustace Hale Ball titled "Trail of the Scarlet Fox."

Another gap of three months. The June 1, 1923, issue lists George W. Sutton, Jr., as the editor, and H. C. North as associate editor.

Nepotism has reared its ugly head. Since the president of the company is A. W. Sutton and the editor is George W. Sutton, Jr., we have to assume that the new editor is the nephew of the president. (Although he might have been the son, brother or possibly even the grandson.)

The September 1, 1923, issue of authors has a brand-new name, although he may have, and probably did, make his first appearance in 1922.

The name is Carroll John Daly.

Although F. M. Osborne held sway over the editorial reins of *Black Mask* for more than three years, his successor, George W. Sutton, Jr., had a shorter reign. He was still editor of the January 1, 1924, issue of *Black Mask*, which featured on the cover "The Seventh Clue" by Dashiell Hammett, author of "It" and "Bodies Piled Up" etc. so he had apparently already published two stories in the magazines.

We don't know George W. Sutton's ability as an editor, but nepotism or not, he was the first editor to publish the redoubtable Dashiell Hammett—and he continued to feature Carroll John Daly.

Sutton published another Dashiell Hammett story, "The Man Who Killed Don Odoms" in the January 15,

1924, issue. This same issue carried a story by a name to become very prominent in other fields of writing, Ben Lucien Burman.

Sometime during the next three months, however, George W. Sutton, Jr., must have incurred the wrath of his uncle or brother, or whoever the relative was, for he has lost his job. The new editor is—P. C. Cody; the associate is still H. C. North. A. W. Sutton remains president of the company. Both Hammett and Daly are featured in the issue.

A gap now of sixteen months. The August, 1925, issue of *Black Mask*. P. C. Cody is the editor, H. C. North is the associate. Carroll John Daly has the lead story in the issue, but a new name appears fifth on the contents page, Erle Stanley Gardner. He has already appeared in the magazine previously and may have cracked the magazine sometime during 1924.

In March, 1926, P. C. Cody is still editor, but no assistant is named so H. C. North has apparently departed for greener pastures. Dashiell Hammett has a story in the issue as does one R. F. Whitfield and one by a brand-new name, Lewis Nebel.

The magazine is again a monthly.

Ready! The November, 1926, issue of *Black Mask* contains the name of a new editor, Joseph T. Shaw. The editor's name is more prominently featured and is in larger and blacker type than formerly.

The new president of Pro-Distributors Publishing Corp. is Eltinge Warner. Apparently he has bought the controlling interest in the corporation. P. C. Cody, however, remains as vice-president. He has relinquished the job of editor, however, and returned to being director of circulation.

Among the contributors in this issue are Carroll John Daly, Frederick Lewis Nebel, Raoul Falconnier Whitfield and Erle Stanley Gardner. A memorable issue.

Get ready for *this* one! The December, 1926, issue. Erle Stanley Gardner and Raoul Falconnier Whitfield are featured in a magazine which has a cowboy on the cover. A brand new author has joined the ranks of *Black Mask* contributors. His name is "Capt. Shaw."

The story is entitled "Makings," a real blood and gore western story.

Sample dialogue:

"Yuh stinkin' bull ain't goin' tuh git away without tryin' to tell yuh again, Larry?"

Honest Injun!

The trend from an all-detective magazine to one of western and adventure has been gradual. It had been originated apparently by Phil Cody, for the cover illustration of the April, 1924, issue was a western one.

Western covers appeared with greater frequency. The new editor, Shaw, not only carried out this western shift but emphasized it during the next few years. There were more western covers on the magazine in 1927 than there were mystery or detective. Strictly western authors began to appear in the magazine. Stephen Payne, a regular contributor to *Ranch Romances* appeared in the magazine in 1928. Other Western writers followed,

132

L. R. Sherman, Eugene Cunningham, although Cunningham also wrote adventure and mystery stories, but was best known as a western writer.

In September, 1928—are you ready for this? . . . there was a real shocker. On a strictly western cover there appeared the title of the lead story, "The Devil's Deputy," by . . .

Are you *really* ready for this?

Erle Stanley Gardner!

The story is a humdinger of a western, featuring Black Barr, gunslinger extraordinary.

Black Barr returned at least once more in a later issue.

Away back in 1927 the February issue, in fact, Nels Leroy Jorgenson had already gone the western route with a story entitled "The Staton Rancho."

Nineteen hundred and twenty-eight was a vintage year. Almost every issue featured the work of Dashiell Hammett, Carroll John Daly, Raoul Whitfield, Frederick Nebel and Nels Leroy Jorgenson. Some issues contained stories by no less than four of these worthies.

Nineteen hundred and twenty-nine was the year of apogee. Hammett, Gardner, Daly, Whitfield, Nebel and Jorgenson dominated the magazine.

Until that fateful September issue. The cover featured a story entitled "The Maltese Falcon" by Dashiell Hammett. The title page added, "*The Saga of a Private Detective.*"

Also in the issue were stories by Gardner, Nebel,

Whitfield, a western by Eugene Cunningham and the first appearance of a brand-new author, who was to become very big, Horace McCoy.

"The Maltese Falcon" ran through four issues. The issue following the January, 1930, contained a novelette by Hammett, "The Farewell Murder." It also contained the first installment of a two-part story, "Green Ice" by Raoul Whitfield, which some authorities say runs "The Maltese Falcon" a close second for the "best mystery ever published in the United States."

Dashiell Hammett did not retire on his laurels. He was out of the February issue of 1930, but he came back in the March issue with "The Glass Key," the first of two parts. The subsequent installment was titled "The Cyclone Shot."

The *Black Mask* writers were really hot in 1929 and 1930, but they had to look to their laurels in 1931, for in the February, 1931, issue appeared the first installment of a four-part serial by an author who had made his debut in the magazine as early as 1926.

The story was titled "The Derelict," and was by Joseph T. Shaw.

In the parlance of 1967, "The Derelict" was a bomb!

Chapter Nineteen

When I first began to read *Black Mask* the giants of the magazine were Dashiell Hammett, Raoul Whitfield, Erle Stanley Gardner, Carroll John Daly and Frederick Nebel. They appeared in the magazine more often than other writers and they were my own favorites.

These authors *were Black Mask.*

Raymond Chandler did not arrive on the scene until 1932.

In the very early years *Black Mask* published many, many authors whose names, whose work did not survive. Of those who survived, the five stalwarts I have named did more, in my estimation, to "make" the magazine and develop the *Black Mask* style of writing than all the other writers put together.

Carroll John Daly was the first of these Big Five to appear in the magazine as early as 1922. Dashiell Hammett came next and soon afterwards Erle Stanley Gardner entered the scene. Both Raoul Whitfield and Frederick Nebel were established by the fall of 1926, when Joseph T. Shaw assumed the editorial reins of *Black Mask.*

It is to Shaw's credit that he encouraged and continued to publish Daly, Hammett, Gardner, Whitfield and Nebel, but that he "discovered" them, that *he* developed the *Black Mask* style of writing is sheer nonsense.

It was handed to him on a silver platter and he was keen enough to polish it with a soft chamois cloth and thus retain its original luster.

The chief criticism I have heard of Shaw—from writers who worked for him—was that he tried to Hammettize the magazine after the success of *The Maltese Falcon*. This received a bit of a setback, however, when the publishers prepared an elaborate circular which was mailed to all the subscribers. The readers were asked to vote on their favorite authors. The result of the poll was:

1. Carroll John Daly
2. Erle Stanley Gardner
3. Dashiell Hammett

I have in my writing lifetime published roughly four hundred stories. I have written fifty-three novels and I have turned out sixty-five feature motion picture screenplays (and believe me, the writing of a feature motion picture is equal to the work of three novels) and perhaps a hundred television scripts.

I have written at least a hundred and fifty articles.

I have written western stories, mysteries, fantasy and science fiction, I have produced love stories and spicy stories. I have turned out reams of Sunday School stories. I have written virtually every type of writing that is published today and some that is no longer being published.

I have written perhaps as much as any living American writer.

No editor has ever given me a plot or the smallest hint of an idea. No editor has ever contributed anything to any of my writing. No editor has ever *taught* me anything. Oh, they've criticized me and at times made me rewrite things, and I did it. But that was *their* opinion, nothing else. They may not necessarily have been right. My version may have been just as good, perhaps, probably better.

I do not believe that one single editor has ever contributed anything to the craft or skill of any single writer at any time.

No editor has ever stood over the shoulder of any writer and told him to write this, use that word, then that one.

Only the writer can write his story.

The writer works out his ideas. He puts the words down on paper. Then he submits his story. The editor buys the story, or rejects it.

He is a *good* editor if he can recognize a good story.

Nobody, absolutely nobody, taught Carroll John Daly how to write. Nobody taught Dashiell Hammett, Erle Stanley Gardner, Raoul Whitfield or Frederick Nebel.

They taught themselves. Perhaps their early stories were rough. A beginning boxer may be clumsy. Continued practice will improve him. Continual practice gives a writer facility, stimulates him, improves his work. But it is he alone who improves himself.

Look at the several hundred writers who appeared in the early issues of *Black Mask*. They fell by the wayside. They weren't skilled enough, did not improve themselves sufficiently to withstand the challenge of the new writers.

There is equality of opportunity. There is no equality of talent. Some people are blessed with it, some are not. Some men can run a mile in four minutes, others cannot do it in forty minutes. One man grows to be six feet in height, another stops at four feet, eleven.

Put one hundred children into one grammar school. Keep them together through grade school, through high school, through college. Some of them will become brilliant scientists, famous doctors or lawyers, successful business men. One or two may become priests. One or two may become thieves or murderers.

Some of the hundred will wind up working in filling stations.

One of the hundred may live to be a hundred. One may die of cancer at the age of twenty-two. One may step off the curb, fall and break his skull. Another may fly an airplane, crash and walk away from it.

The man who invented the typewriter was a creator. The man who sells it is a salesman.

The writer is a creator. The editor is not. Neither is the printer, the bookbinder or the clerk in the book store who sells the book to the consumer.

They are all necessary, yes, but to each his job. Accept it.

The mania for higher education will one day destroy our civilization. In another generation virtually every adult will be a college graduate.

Who, then, will collect our garbage, clean our streets?

Who will construct those streets and roads?

Who will build our houses? The architect will be a college graduate and he will design the house, but who will dig the foundations, who will lay the bricks, carry the mortar, nail the boards and shingle the roof?

A college graduate?

Will college graduates drive our busses, deliver our mail, chop our meat, check out our groceries in the supermarket?

The opportunity for a college education should be there, but it should be for those who want it badly enough, for those who will benefit from it.

It should not be a refuge from work. It should not be to keep people off the labor market.

If a youth has certain talent and the desire to become someone, he should go to college. If he has no talent whatever, no desire to be anything, he should drop out of school and get a job in a filling station. Why wait until he is out of college to start pumping gas? If he starts young enough he will know how to change tires by the time the other potential filling station lad gets out of college. Changing tires is a necessary thing in our way of life.

*   *   *

Joseph Shaw was a *good* editor. He loved *Black Mask* and he enjoyed the society of authors. He was exceedingly proud of the contributors who appeared in his magazine. He always found time to talk to authors, those who sold to him and those who aspired to do so.

He introduced many new writers to his magazine. He published the first work of Raymond Chandler. He did not "discover" him. A story by Raymond Chandler was submitted to *Black Mask* and Shaw was a good enough editor to recognize a good story and a good writer. He did not "make" Chandler. Chandler made himself.

Carroll John Daly became one of my closest friends. He lived in White Plains when we lived in Scarsdale, four miles away. We visited back and forth, sometimes two and three times a week. He was my type of man and his wife and mine got along well together. We talked much about writing. He told me of his early days as a writer.

He talked much of Harry North as an "editor," although the facts of life indicate that H. C. North was never more than an associate editor. He mentioned Sutton, but not as often as North. He had a very high regard for Phil Cody as an editor. Daly wrote for *Black Mask* from 1922 until around 1940. He contributed to the magazine for four years under the editorship of Osborne, Sutton, Cody, ten years of Captain Shaw's tenure and four years under the editorship of Fanny Ellsworth.

Perhaps he worked too long, wrote too much for

Shaw. He never really criticized him, but he was almost always cool in his mention of him.

Besides contributing to *Black Mask*, Daly wrote a great deal for *Detective Fiction Weekly*, mostly under the editorship of Howard Bloomfield. He contributed frequently to *Dime Detective*, which paid him four cents a word, a cent a word more than *Black Mask* paid him.

However, when *Black Mask* declined, Daly's writing career declined. He had developed a style of writing that he found hard to change. The *Black Mask* style of writing lost its vogue in the late thirties and early forties. Daly's career suffered. He finally left New York and moved to California. He lived for a while in Santa Monica, where I saw him once or twice, then he and his wife moved to Coachella, in the desert. Toward the end of his career he had become reduced to writing for the comic books.

Several years ago a secondhand magazine dealer showed me two copies of *Breezy Stories*, vintage 1922. Each contained a story by Erle Stanley Gardner. He, too, tried everything before he found his metier. I sent the magazine to Gardner and he wrote me a warm letter in reply.

Erle has had an extremely long writing career. He was first published in 1922 and now, forty-five years later he is still at it. And writing as well, if not better than he ever did.

Dashiell Hammett had a comparatively short writing career. He first appeared in *Black Mask* in 1923. He wrote his last work in 1932, "The Thin Man." He never published a line after 1932, yet he lived until 1960. This is one of the imponderables that has caused me to wonder about every now and then. He was at the apogee of his career in 1932. Why did he quit abruptly?

His income from his writing did not stop in 1932, by any means. MGM paid him every time they made a Thin Man picture. He drew substantial royalties from the Sam Spade radio show, from "The Fat Man," from the continual reissues of his books, his shorter material.

I have recently read Lillian Hellman's long introduction to the Hammett collection published under the title, *The Big Knockover*. That Hammett and Lillian Hellman were close for many years was no secret. When Hammett stopped writing, Lillian Hellman began. She went on to become one of our most successful playwrights. The thought occurs that Hammett may have devoted much of his time to helping Hellman. But there is no similarity whatever in the writing of Hellman and Hammett.

I don't know what happened to Raoul Whitfield. He was one of my real favorites in *Black Mask*, but I never met him. He stopped writing about 1932 or 1933. He married an extremely wealthy woman, lived near Las Vegas, Nevada, for a long time. His wife was mysteriously murdered. I have read some rather lurid accounts of it in the "true" detective magazines. The murder was never solved, but Whitfield stopped writing about this time.

I met Frederick Nebel only once. It was in the office

of *Dime Detective*. He turned out to be a rather small, mild man. He quit writing for the pulps about 1935. His eyes were on the women's quality magazines, which paid very high rates and used quieter, less violent stories than Nebel was accustomed to writing. But this is what he seemed to want. I saw his name in the women's magazines through the years, but his fame never reached the heights it did in *Black Mask*. And I believe his *Black Mask* contributions will outlive his later writing.

Raymond Chandler was a comparative late-comer. When he first appeared in *Black Mask* in 1932 he was a man of forty-five or so. Although he lived for another thirty years, his writing production was comparatively meager. He was a continual rewriter. Six books, a couple of dozen novelettes comprised his total writing production.

I had a fight with Chandler in 1946 and he would never speak to me afterwards. We had the same Hollywood agent, H. N. Swanson, and we would run into each other continuously, but he always looked through me when we met.

In 1946, Chandler had a squabble with my pal, Steve Fisher, over a screenplay credit, "The Lady in the Lake," made by MGM. Steve won the Guild arbitration. Shortly thereafter, Paramount gave a party to promote "The Blue Dahlia," an original screenplay that Chandler had written. I was one of those invited. Chandler saw me, came across the room and snarled at me that I was a buddy of Fisher's, the dirty so-and-so . . .

I cut him off, told him yes Steve was my best friend.

Chandler continued his tirade and I let him have it. In 1946, Chandler was in his late fifties, or early sixties, and I was only forty-two and still in pretty good physical condition. Chandler sensed what was about to happen if he persisted, I guess, and broke it off abruptly.

However, this did not prevent me from enjoying Raymond Chandler's writing. I have always liked his work tremendously and have reread much of it. I liked *The Long Goodbye*, which was published some time after our little tiff, about as well as any of Chandler's writings.

Anent this, I had to be held back physically to keep from smacking down a bantam writer back in New York in 1941. I still read his books and enjoy them. My son is a great fan of this writer and accumulated a lot of his books. I did not read them for some years, but when I was in the hospital in 1957 Bob brought me about a dozen of this writer's books and I read them all and enjoyed them very much.

* * *

The *Black Mask* "School of Writing."

Life in the United States in 1920 moved at an accelerated pace. The leisurely life of the pre-war days was gone. People who had been social drinkers only before Prohibition now became heavy drinkers, merely because it was against the law. F. Scott Fitzgerald was the literary spokesman of The Jazz Age, "the lost generation."

A group of expatriates had settled down on the Left Bank in Paris and were trying to create a new form of literary expression. In the United States, Sinclair Lewis was tearing down the strongholds of conservatism of small-town life, of the "small-town mind," of the business and professional men of the cities.

Hemingway was groping for recognition in Paris. He was not getting it. He was a correspondent for a provincial newspaper in Canada. He wrote plotless short stories, some of which sold, some of which did not.

In the United States, writers were trying to inject more realism into their stories. They stripped them of verbiage, blue-penciled the descriptive passages, kept their stories moving. The characters became strong, silent men. The stories became more violent, the prose became sparser.

In *Black Mask* a group of writers were showing how this could be done. The several early editors gave their contributors a free rein. Writers in other magazines were imitating the writers of *Black Mask*, but *Black Mask* had rounded up the best practitioners of the new style and kept them happy.

At its best, *Black Mask* published the sparsest prose of any magazine in the country. Joe Shaw used to admonish his new writers, "Prune and cut, don't use a single word that you can do without. Read Hammett, Gardner, Nebel, Daly. Try to write like them."

The *Black Mask* writers did. So did many, many other writers. Hemingway's style, when he finally found it in *The Sun Also Rises* and *A Farewell to Arms*, is right out of *Black Mask*. Even though he never published anything in the magazine, he most certainly read it. As did James M. Cain and many other writers.

The only taboos in *Black Mask* were those of good taste. A man could swear (although not four-letter words). He could go to bed with a woman not his wife. He could kick a man in the teeth. He could bleed and he could suffer, although he had to suffer in silence.

You could even have a Negro villain. Dashiell Hammett, who later made no bones about the fact that he was a Marxist, had Negro villains in several stories and he called them by names that would today bring the Civil Rights groups down upon him.

The Maltese Falcon, published in book form by Knopf, immediately after its appearance in *Black Mask*, was a tremendous success, going through something like fourteen printings. Yet it was sold to Warner Brothers for around five thousand dollars. A film was made of it starring Ricardo Cortez as Sam Spade, with Bebe Daniels playing the part that Mary Astor did so well in the 1940 remake. The fat man, later played by Sydney Greenstreet, was played in the earlier version by Dudley Digges. I saw the picture when I was living in Iowa in 1931 and thought it was a wonderful film.

Yet the 1940 version with Humphrey Bogart was even better.

Chandler's success with motion pictures was less than spectacular in the early years. He sold *Farewell My Lovely* to RKO for two thousand dollars. They made it into a "Saint" picture. He sold *The High Window* to Fox for two thousand dollars and it was made with George Montgomery. His books did not click in Hollywood until Howard Hawks paid twenty thousand dollars for *The Big Sleep*, and the picture came off very well. RKO then remade *Farewell My Lovely* with Richard Powell and it was a smash hit. But Chandler got no additional money. Neither did he get paid again when Fox remade *The High Window*. However, MGM bought *Lady in the Lake* for thirty-five thousand dollars and Chandler was then "discovered" by Hollywood.

Chapter Twenty

Nineteen hundred and thirty-eight.

I was in big at *Short Stories*, at *Ranch Romances* and at *Black Mask*. I was in solid at Street & Smith and had a verbal contract to deliver a story a week at one and three-quarters cents a word. I could pick the pulp magazines for which I wanted to write.

I wanted to get out of the pulps.

Steve Fisher was making it in the slicks, although he still continued to write for the pulps. I decided to see if I could get into the slicks, although the type of stories they published were not to my especial liking. But you had to progress. I had licked *Black Mask* and where else was there to go?

I picked on *Liberty* as my first slick. I studied the magazine for several weeks, then sat down and wrote a short story. I sent it to the offices of *Liberty* in the MacFadden Building. The story was rejected with a brief note.

I was not satisfied and having the experience of the pulps behind me, decided to make a personal onslaught on the editor, Oscar Graeve, who had been editor of *Delineator* for years before assuming the editorial post at *Liberty*.

I called at the office and the receptionist tried to brush me off. I refused to be brushed. She wanted to summon an assistant. I said no, it had to be the editor or no one. I recited my credits, perhaps embellished them a little. Wonder of wonders, she relayed the information and Oscar Graeve said he would see me. I went in and gave him a really good sales pitch, leaving the manuscript with him, which he promised he would read personally.

The manuscript was in the morning mail. Mr. Graeve had read it immediately, but had decided that it was not good enough for *Liberty*.

I was still not satisfied.

I scouted around a day or two; and obtained the home address of Fulton Oursler, who had written a few books himself and was editorial director-in-chief of *Liberty* and all the other MacFadden Magazines. I sent the manuscript to his home at West Falmouth, Massachusetts. He did his editorial work by teletype and about two quick trips a month to New York. I wrote a letter with the manuscript, told Oursler about myself, what I had written, what I hoped to accomplish.

The next day I received a long-distance phone call from West Falmouth, Massachusetts.

Oursler was buying the story. Not only that but he wanted to see me in New York the following week!

Later, I wrote another story for *Liberty*. I wrote it in

149

two hours, seventeen pages. I sent it to *Liberty*, first draft, without a word of rewriting or correction. They bought it for five hundred dollars. Several years later I sold the story to RKO for ten thousand dollars; the best-paid two hours' work in my entire life.

The slicks did not satisfy me. I read the magazines and did not like the stories. Most of them were terribly effeminate, it seemed to me, and I was more at home with the virile, masculine type of story. Also I had become a novelette writer in the pulps and my thoughts ran more along the lines of longer, more complex stories.

*   *   *

Obviously, I should write a book.

The decision to do so was not an easy one to make. The book market in the late 1930's was not good. The retail price of a mystery or western novel was two dollars. The sales of both mysteries and westerns was small. I had read somewhere that Erle Stanley Gardner's first Perry Mason novel, published in 1932, had sold thirty-eight hundred copies, which was considered a very good sale. But at twenty cents a copy the royalties for the book were only seven hundred and sixty dollars.

I asked around. The average mystery novel sold under two thousand copies. The smaller houses bought them for flat sums, anywhere between one hundred and two hundred and fifty dollars.

Westerns, brr! They were chiefly rental library items. Twelve hundred copies was the average sale. Advances at the better houses were two hundred and fifty dollars and the book seldom earned more than that. One rental library publisher, in fact, paid a flat one hundred fifty dollars per book, FOR ALL RIGHTS. I knew a writer who had a contract with them for six western books a year at one hundred and fifty dollars a book. The six books took his entire time and netted him nine hundred dollars a year. I was averaging better than a thousand dollars a month from the pulps.

Motion pictures? Almost no western novels sold to motion pictures. Only a very few mysteries sold and usually for very low prices, two hundred and fifty to five hundred dollars. *Black Mask* writers now and then sold a mystery to pictures for those prices.

Yet Erle Stanley Gardner's books had hit. His sales had gone 'way, 'way up. And *Liberty* was buying the serial rights to the Perry Mason books.

Ernest Haycox had been an exceedingly good pulp writer and had made it in the slicks with his serials, which later were published in book form.

Luke Short, a pulp writer, was making it in the slicks with his serials.

Rex Stout was writing mystery novels, Erle Stanley Gardner was whacking them out regularly, Jonathan Latimer was doing nicely with them. Ellery Queen was turning out great books. So was Kurt Steel and a number of other mystery writers. Too, too many of them.

There were fifty good mystery novel writers.

There seemed to be only two readable western novelists. Ernest Haycox and Luke Short.

I knew Haycox from correspondence. More than a year before I had become dissatisfied with the type of westerns I was writing. It seemed to me my stories were on the artificial side and I concluded that I did not know enough about the West. I had read some of Haycox's pulp stories and I got a number of his books and was fascinated with them. Authenticity rang from every page. The man was a superb writer, too.

I wrote him a letter, told him my problems. He wrote back and suggested a number of factual western books that might be of help. He gave me the name of a rare book dealer in New York from whom I might obtain these books. I spent two hundred dollars at this dealer's on my first visit. I crammed the books and an entire new world opened up to me. I began to *study* the West. I kept up a correspondence with Haycox.

I may already have had in the back of my mind the thought that I would one day write western books and hoped to become one-half as good as Ernest Haycox was.

Now, in 1938, after having surveyed both the western book and serial market and the mystery book and serial market, I made the decision to try a western novel.

I wrote *Peace Marshal* in three weeks.

I knew the magazine editors and the magazines. I did not know the book editors or the book publishing business. I had not used an agent since The Human Encyclopedia fiasco two years previously. Everyone I talked to said you had to have a top agent to break into the book field. I asked around, narrowed down the list of potential agents and finally chose one. I went up and talked to the agent and he turned me over to an assistant who handled the book sales. I gave him *Peace Marshal*. Three weeks went by and I was fuming. I was used to overnight reading by editors. I phoned the agent. He said he was writing me a letter. It came.

It was a flat turndown. *Peace Marshal* would not sell to any book publisher, not even the cheap, rental library publishers who were buying western books for one hundred and fifty dollars each. All rights.

It would not sell as a serial to even the half-cent a word pulps. I was wasting my time trying to write books. Period.

Although I knew virtually every pulp magazine editor in New York by this time, there was one whom I had never met, Howard Bloomfield, editor of *Adventure*. In the general adventure field, *Adventure* stood head and shoulders above the field.

I went up and met Howard Bloomfield for the first time. He said little, showed very little interest in my sales pitch. He would read the story in a week.

The following Friday I went back to *Adventure*. Howard said he had just finished reading *Peace Marshal* and would like to buy it. Twelve hundred dollars. He did not ask for a single word of revision!

I now made a momentous decision. Twelve hundred dollars was the largest sum of money I had ever had at one time in my life. I still had that gnawing frustration about Hollywood. Why not invest the money in a trip to Hollywood and get it out of my mind once and for all?

I submitted a carbon copy of *Peace Marshal* to the William Morrow Company, who seemed to publish about the best westerns being put out at the time.

We had a new Buick and even though it was early December, we started driving westward. We stopped at St. Louis and my mother-in-law decided to take the trip with us. We drove to California, and when we got there I consulted a road map and saw that I could go by Temecula without driving too far out of the way.

Temecula was the home of Erle Stanley Gardner. I had never met him before.

He greeted me warmly and almost the first thing he said was that Morrow was taking *Peace Marshal.* Thayer Hobson had mentioned it in a letter.

I spent a week in Hollywood and visited many of the pulp writers I knew only through reputation: Norbert Davis, John K. Butler, Cleve F. Adams, Harry Olmsted, W. T. Ballard and many others. I had no Hollywood entree and met no one from the picture business.

I decided that I should have a Hollywood agent and went up to see H. N. Swanson. I gave him The Human Encyclopedia stories and told him the long, sad story.

*　　*　　*

We got back to New York the day after Christmas and found a telegram waiting from H. N. Swanson. Telephone him. I did. He had sold the Human Encyclopedia stories to Paramount Pictures for twenty-five hundred dollars.

I spent less than a week in New York and then drove back to California. Swanson got me a one-week job at

Republic Studios for three hundred dollars a week. He got me an assignment immediately afterwards at Paramount on a western story on which there had been seventeen writers before me. I lasted three weeks before the very confused producer closed me out.

I sat around Hollywood for several weeks, hoping to get another job. Swanson could not get one for me. I met a few people, found that magazine writers were not taken too seriously in Hollywood. Book writers? Ah, yes . . . but not western book writers. Western books were bought for from two hundred and fifty to five hundred dollars.

Chapter Twenty-one

We had an apartment at the Sunset Towers and I made the decision to write a mystery novel. I bought about fifty mystery novels and read them day and night. I liked the tremendous pace and plots of the Perry Mason novels, but I enjoyed thoroughly the humor of the Jonathan Latimer books. I decided to write a mystery with the complex plot and pace of a Gardner book, but add the humor of Jonathan Latimer.

I wrote one-half of *The French Key* in three days, then got bogged down for a week and could not write a word. I got back at it then and finished the story in another four days. Total writing time, seven days, but during a two-week period. I had Massey's Manuscript Service type up the manuscript and sent the original to Morrow in New York. While I was debating about taking the other copies to Swanson I read a fantastic item in the Hollywood trade papers. Bill Dozier, the story agent for Berg-Allenberg Agency, had just sold a "first" mystery, *Send Another Coffin* for ten thousand dollars. *Send Another Coffin* had just been published by the William Morrow Company.

I took a copy of the script to Dozier. A week went by and I called on Dozier. Yes, he had read the story. What did he think of it? He refused to say. I had submitted the story to Morrow. If Thayer Hobson took it on he, Bill Dozier, would give it his very best efforts. But what if Morrow turned down the story?

In that case he, Bill Dozier, would not handle *The French Key*. (I got even with Bill Dozier years later. I took him for ninety dollars playing gin rummy.)

I was irate, but did not know what to do. I would have to sweat it out. I sent a copy of the story to Dorothy McIlwraith of *Short Stories*. Another week went by.

A letter from Thayer Hobson. A long letter rejecting *The French Key*. Bill Dozier turned it back to me. But the same day came a wire from Dorothy McIlwraith. She would like to use *The French Key* as a serial in *Short Stories*.

I said the hell with Hollywood and drove back to New York. There I learned that Farrar & Rinehart had announced the Mary Roberts Rinehart Mystery Novel Contest.

I went up cold, got in to talk to Jean Crawford, an associate editor. I gave her a sales pitch, left a copy of *The French Key*.

I saw Howard Bloomfield and he asked me to write another serial for *Adventure*. I wrote *Quantrell's Flag* and he bought it, again without revision.

*　　*　　*

A phone call from Farrar & Rinehart. Would I come in and talk to John Farrar? I could scarcely wait until the next day.

I was summoned into the sanctum and met Stanley Rinehart, John Farrar, Fred Rinehart and several of the staff members, inculding Jean Crawford. The contest still had a week to run, but they had already read three hundred and eighty-five manuscripts and had picked mine as the best of the entire lot!

While it was still unofficial, it looked like I had won the contest! At any rate, they wanted to give me a contract for *The French Key* and discuss a regular program. They had looked into my writing background and thought that I would become a valuable mystery novelist.

By the damndest coincidence I ran into Thayer Hobson on the street after leaving Farrar & Rinehart's offices. Gleefully I told him that I had just won the Mary Roberts Rinehart Mystery Novel Contest.

He went into a rage, said that I had had no right to submit *The French Key* to Farrar & Rinehart. The book had been sent to him and *he* was going to publish it.

I was astounded. He had rejected the story! No sir, he had merely made some suggestions for revision, that was all. I went home, reread Hobson's letter to me. It was as flat a rejection as I had ever read. True, there had been mention of things that were wrong with the story, but Hobson had not asked me to change them, or rewrite in any shape or form.

I phoned him. He admitted that he had read the carbon of his letter and conceded that the letter was a turndown. He had not meant it to be, but I was quite right. I could have construed it as such and he would say no more.

A few days later I received a jolt from Farrar & Rinehart. I had not won the contest, after all!

A last-minute entry by a woman writer had won. However, I was given Honorable Mention, along with three other writers.

The "winner" of the Mary Roberts Rinehart Mystery Novel contest was published several months after *The French Key*.

It died lousy in the streets.

At the end of the year *The French Key* was on every list of "Best Mysteries of 1940." The winner of the contest failed to make a single list!

Chapter Twenty-two

In 1939 a new factor entered the book publishing business. A company called Pocket Books, Inc., headed by Robert de Graff, put out a line of little paperback books with laminated covers. They were excellently printed and the stories were well chosen.

The books appeared on the newsstands with absolutely no fanfare. The publishing world seemed to be more or less indifferent to them. The initial printings were only between thirty thousand and fifty thousand copies and the books sold for twenty-five cents. The authors were paid one cent a copy royalties, but the publishers who had leased the rights took half of this. So, at most the publishers got two hundred and fifty dollars in "found" money and the author got that much. Nothing to get really excited about. It was a fad and would soon blow away.

But Pocket Books caught on. Bob de Graff increased his print orders to one hundred thousand copies and the books were sellouts. Advances for stories went up to a thousand dollars.

I had lunch one day with Bill Weber, who was the advertising manager of Scribner's, but on the side, as Jack Ketch, reviewed mystery novels for the daily *New York Herald-Tribune* and under the name of Judge Lynch for the *Saturday Review of Literature*. His reviews were higly regarded and he led the parade in his praise of *The French Key*.

As we left the restaurant we met Bob de Graff. Weber introduced me to him and de Graff told me that he had read *The French Key* and had approached Farrar & Rinehart about doing it in paperback. Someone at Farrar & Rinehart had told him that one cent a copy royalty was inadequate, that they wouldn't let him have *The French Key* for less than two cents a copy royalty. De Graff assured me that no one got more than the one cent royalty, that he could not afford to pay more.

The hard book publishers were resisting the encroachment of the paperback books. They did not like them and they did everything to make their lot difficult. It was like the major motion picture studios resisting the advent of television in the late 1940's. Instead of embracing it they permitted independents to take it over—and prosper.

A few months later a company named Avon Books issued a line of paperback titles. The books were crudely printed and offered slight competition to Pocket Books. Still, they sold. They bought *The French Key*, *The Hungry Dog* and *Simon Lash* and paid a thousand dollars advance for each.

A short time after Avon began, Ian Ballantine came

from England to establish an American branch of Penguin Books. He brought with him two assistants, Dr. Kurt Enoch and Victor Weybright. I visited them in their first office, which had as a staff, besides the three men, a single secretary.

Ballantine could not have been much over twenty-five at this time. He looked years younger than Enoch and Weybright, who were probably in their early forties. But Ballantine was the boss.

I was one of Penguin's first authors. The books they brought out were different in appearance than those of Pocket Books, but they were excellently designed and printed.

The three partners later bought out the American branch of Penguin and changed its name to New American Library of World Literature. The books they issued were called Signet and Mentor Books. In 1944, Ian Ballantine left New American Library to organize a brand new company, Bantam Books.

Paper quotas had been frozen during the war. The several paperback companies that had begun publication after Pocket Books, Avon and Penguin were forced to limit their editions to one hundred thousand copies. So, too, were the three leaders. But with paper quotas lifted at the close of the war, when Bantam Books made their appearance, the paperback business exploded.

I couldn't believe it, when Rinehart told me that one of the first four books to be issued by the new Bantam Books Company was to be my book, *The Gift Horse*, and that the advance would be four thousand dollars!

The book, incidentally, sold three hundred and forty-one thousand copies. Ballantine left Bantam Books after a very few years to organize Ballantine Books, which he still heads.

I visited the offices of New American Library after the war and there were not less than two hundred people working there. A fast jump from the staff of four in 1940!

But all of this is looking ahead. In 1940, the paperback book business was still very much touch and go. Five hundred dollars for an author's share of the royalties was all right, but it did not greatly augment a writer's income, not a writer who was used to earning fifteen hundred to two thousand dollars a month and who was spending that much.

Chapter Twenty-three

The customary advance on a mystery novel in 1939 was only two hundred and fifty dollars, which was what I received from Farrar & Rinehart for *The French Key*. I expected that the book would earn me another two hundred and fifty or three hundred dollars, but I had not forgotten that ten thousand dollars that Bill Dozier had received for that "first" mystery novel and I still had strong hopes of selling *The French Key* to pictures.

It would be several months, however, before the book would be published and I had to keep on earning money. I wrote a second Johnny Fletcher novel, *The Laughing Fox*. I sold the serial rights to *Short Stories*, for which I also wrote two or three long novelettes.

I wrote a couple of stories for *Black Mask* and several fifteen-thousand to twenty-five-thousand-word stories for John Nanovic, who had taken over *Clues* from F. Orlin Tremaine. My records indicate that I also wrote three Jim Strong stories for Street & Smith during this period, plus a twenty-five-thousand-word "novel" for *Ranch Romances*.

I was grinding it out.

February, 1940.

The French Key was published and the reviews began to come in. I subscribed to a clipping service. Of some one hundred and seventy-five reviews only two were bad. Most of the reviews were as good as if I had written them myself. The book went into a quick second printing. It sold over forty-five hundred copies—which was seven hundred more than Erle Stanley Gardner's first book had sold.

Lois was pregnant during this period. After *The French Key* we had decided that it was time to settle down permanently and start raising a family.

Bob was born on August 11, 1940, the day *The Laughing Fox* was published. I recall that I got an advance from Farrar & Rinehart to pay the obstetrician and the hospital bill.

The reception of *The French Key* was all that any mystery writer could ask for. I wrote a note to Walter Winchell, telling him how I had learned about a "French" key and he printed a "New York Novelette" in his column, which was very big in those days.

Within a week after the publication of *The French Key* I was overwhelmed to receive from Farrar & Rinehart a card written to me, in care of them, from William Lyon Phelps.

The dean of all literary critics for many years was William Lyon Phelps. It was said that a favorable review from Phelps "made" a book. When I first got to know Carroll John Daly he showed me several reviews that Phelps had done on his *Black Mask* stories, published in book form in the late twenties and early thirties. Phelps had called Daly the best of the mystery writers.

This card that I now received from Phelps had scrawled on it: ". . . *The French Key is the best of eight thousand murder stories I have read.*"

I was bowled over, but Phelps continued writing me notes for several years and he reviewed my books in *Esquire* and other magazines and never failed to give me glowing reviews. I finally met him in 1941 at the Ellery Queen party to celebrate the one-hundredth anniversary of the *Detective Story*. Phelps was seventy-two years old at the time. He put his arm about my shoulder and talked to me and I was so choked with emotion I could scarcely answer. It made up for all those meals I had missed back in 1934.

*   *   *

If I had worked hard in the previous years, I worked twice as hard in 1940. I wrote *The Laughing Fox, The Talking Clock, The Hungry Dog* and *Simon Lash* for Farrar & Rinehart.

I sold the first serial rights to *The Talking Clock* to *Detective Fiction Weekly* and the others to *Short Stories*.

I wrote *Outlaw* for *Adventure*. I wrote three or four novels for *Ranch Romances* and several long novelettes for *Clues*. I wrote novelettes for *Short Stories*, for *Black Mask* and *Detective Fiction Weekly*.

Farrar & Rinehart published *Outlaw* in book form

and it sold one thousand eight hundred fifty copies, in spite of really good reviews.

The enchantment of western books was suddenly gone. I decided to write no more.

I poured it on in 1940, producing more than eight hundred thousand words. The more I wrote, the more I *had* to write. I was making commitments all over town and I had to deliver.

In spite of my decision not to write any more westerns, I committed myself to writing a serial for *Ranch Romances* and whacked out "Gunsight." I thought I would try a new publisher for this one and took it down to Dodd-Mead. I made a deal with them, then somehow talked myself into doing a book for them under a pseudonym. This was *The Yellow Overcoat* by Stephen Acre.

Rinehart was now scheduling four books a year by me, about all they could handle. But I had to write more than this number. I thought I would try another book under a pseudonym. I made a deal with Reynal & Hitchcock. Everyone was sworn to secrecy. Nobody, but nobody, would reveal that Charles K. Boston, the author of *The Silver Jackass*, was really Frank Gruber.

The next day I received a phone call from Stanley Rinehart. "What's this *Silver Jackass* you're writing for Reynal & Hitchcock?"

Everyone had been sworn to secrecy but the sales manager of Reynal & Hitchcock just happened to be a cousin of the sales manager of Farrar & Rinehart.

Well, I had gone this far, I might as well go a little

farther. I contracted with Henry Holt & Company to do *The Last Doorbell* by John K. Vedder.

*   *   *

In 1941 I had to ease off on the regular pulp writing. I don't believe I wrote more than one or two short stories that year and I eased off in *Black Mask* and *Detective Fiction Weekly.*

A new editor took over *Detective Story* at Street & Smith, and offered me a really excellent rate to write some lead novels for the magazine. I undertook them and then John Nanovic, angry I guess because I had gone over to a competitive magazine, even though it was a Street & Smith book, raised my rate and I wrote some more longer stories for him.

I don't think I missed an issue of *Short Stories* that year. If I did not have a serial running in the magazine I had a long novelette.

Bill Delaney, the owner of *Short Stories,* had become one of my best friends. Through him I met Walter J. Black, who had a book club for classics. It was called The Classic Club. I talked to him a number of times and he kept sounding me out about mysteries, but never revealed the reason. Suddenly he announced The Detective Book Club, a mail order operation. This has become, through the years, a very successful thing and a great many of my mysteries have been selections of the club. The first book of mine Black took on was *The Mighty Blockhead.* At that time Black paid one thousand dollars flat royalties to the author, of which the original publisher, however, got half.

Things were adding up, though. Five hundred from

the paperback companies, five hundred from the book club, seven or eight hundred from the original hardcover editions, a couple of hundred from the Grosset & Dunlap seventy-five-cent hardcover editions, one thousand to fifteen hundred dollars for first serial rights; a mystery novel was beginning to earn respectable money.

I still could not sell a book to motion pictures. I had sold The Human Encyclopedia series to Paramount for twenty-five hundred dollars, but there seemed to be a vast indifference to my books in Hollywood. I still had that gnawing frustration about it.

In 1941 Steve Fisher suddenly sold an original to Twentieth Century-Fox and received with it a six months' writing contract. He had hardly arrived in Hollywood than his novel, *I Wake Up Screaming*, was published and he sold it to Fox for seventy-five hundred dollars, a very handsome price for a mystery.

I wrote the pseudonym books in 1941 and for Farrar & Rinehart I wrote *The Mighty Blockhead*, *The Navy Colt*, *The Buffalo Box*. I wrote "Gunsight" for *Ranch Romances*.

I worked as hard in 1941 as I did in 1940 and I was gasping from the pressure of the tremendous amount of wordage I was turning out. I had a bear by the short hairs and I could not let go.

Early in 1942 Stanley Rinehart invited me to lunch. Years ago, when at Doubleday's, they had published Edgar Wallace and he had always thought of "finding" an American Edgar Wallace. He asked if I could write a book a month. I said certainly.

No more was said. I thought it was idle talk. Two

weeks later I was again asked to lunch. The people at Farrar & Rinehart had discussed the subject, had put out feelers with the wholesalers, etc. and they were ready to launch the project.

A book a month by the American Edgar Wallace . . . Frank Gruber.

I had not given the matter too much thought. Actually, with eight hundred thousand words a year, I was already producing the equivalent of twelve books. But now I hedged. I would be willing to take the chance, I told Stanley, if they would hold off announcing it for three months—to give me time to turn out three books so that if I missed a month we could throw in one of these three books.

I began to write the books and it was very, very rough. Now that I had a monthly deadline a mental block began to form. But I could not permit such a thing to happen. I wrote two of the books, was into the third.

Out of a clear sky I received a telegram from Hollywood. Two years ago I had given a copy of *Peace Marshal* to Ned Brown. He had put in his rubber stamp and had left the book at the office of Harry Sherman. I had long ago left the Ned Brown Agency and had virtually forgotten that *Peace Marshal* was in Hollywood. Besides, I had ceased writing western stories and it was from a mystery I expected to get that eventual tap on the shoulder.

Harry Sherman, after two years, had picked up *Peace*

Marshal one day and read it. He was making the Hopalong Cassidy pictures, but made two "specials" a year with Richard Dix. He offered one thousand dollars for the picture rights to *Peace Marshal*.

It was not a bad price. Westerns were still selling in Hollywood for from two hundred fifty to five hundred dollars—and very few were bought. It was cheaper to employ a script writer at seventy-five dollars a week (which was about what the western script writers got in those days) and have them come up with an "original" idea.

I accepted Sherman's offer, but urged Ned Brown to try to get me a writing assignment in addition. He managed it at the last moment, three hundred fifty dollars a week for six weeks.

Hollywood had finally called me!

We had moved from Scarsdale to Manhasset on Long Island in January, 1942. We had a beautiful home, a brand new house with ten rooms and four baths. Our rent was one hundred seventy-five dollars a month. The same house would rent today in Hollywood for one thousand dollars a month. It would sell for around two hundred thousand dollars.

We decided to close up the house, leave everything in it and take the train to Hollywood, carrying only our suitcases—and Bob, who was then twenty-two months of age.

I completed *The Gift Horse* the day before we were due to leave. Bill Delaney came down to the train to see us off and I gave him the last chapters and asked him to have them retyped and send the manuscript to Farrar & Rinehart.

I wrote F & R on the train. I told them I would be back in six weeks, that I needed a vacation.

I did not see New York again until 1946.

Chapter Twenty-four

I have not talked about the terrible loneliness of the writing profession.

Only you, and you alone, can sit down and write those many, many words that are necessary to make a story; your plot, your incidents, your characters and your dialogue.

A five-thousand-word story consists roughly of seventeen typewritten pages. Two hours of steady typing, if you are just copying. But to create seventeen pages of words!

You've got to decide first what kind of story you are going to write. Then you have to work out a plot. Not an idea—one of those brilliant "ideas" that amateurs get continuously and know are better than the trash that's in the magazines.

The real writer has to work out a logical plot—a *complete* plot. A plot with an opening, with scenes that progress and build to a climax and then a smashing finale.

The basic formula of a short story is simple enough:

A protagonist is presented with a problem and your story shows how he solves—or fails to solve—this problem.

In these few words is encompassed a vast amount of detail.

Who is your protagonist?

What is his problem?

How does he solve it (or fail to solve it)?

Who are your other characters? What is the relationship of each—to the protagonist, to the other characters?

What are the incidents?

All of these things have to be faced by the writer before he can sit down and actually write his seventeen pages.

Only the writer alone can work out this myriad of ideas and detail. No one can help him do it. He must do it alone, and he must write down his five thousand words, his seventeen pages.

It may take him two hours, three hours if he is lucky and can concentrate well enough.

It might take him two days or a week. A month.

There are writers who take a week to write a short story. Two weeks is not unknown and I have known writers who work for a solid month on one five-thousand-word short story.

Only the very fortunate writers can sit down and, starting from scratch, write a short story (a short story that will sell) in two or three hours. And they can do it only so often. Sooner or later the pitcher will be taken to the well too often.

174

Only a writer who has endured the writing of a dozen stories, of a hundred, of four hundred, understands the agony that went with those countless hours of mental aberration.

And only a writer who has endured all of it knows about the terrible loneliness.

A writer is truly alone. He sits and thinks, works and reworks his ideas, his thoughts. And then he writes and rewrites. And while he is doing all of this, he is utterly alone.

I am talking of the writing of a short story.

A ten-thousand-word novelette requires a proportionately greater amount of work and thought.

A novel.

A short novel consists of sixty thousand words. The equivalent of twelve short stories?

No.

A short story can be of a single thread, a slight premise revolved around a trick or gimmick. A novel must have scope, it must have importance. Above all it must have an abundance of characters and plot complications.

I have written in my lifetime a vast amount of material. In 1935 I wrote fifty-seven stories and sold fifty-five. About twenty of the stories were five thousand words or less. The rest were longer, so the average length was well over five thousand words.

I wrote fewer stories in subsequent years, but the stories were much longer. The majority of them ran between fifteen thousand and twenty-five thousand words.

I have sold in my writing life four hundred stories. Most of these were written between the years 1934 and 1941. Since 1941 I have written only five or six stories of less than novel length.

I have written fifty-three novels.

I would rather write twenty-four short stories than one novel—from the standpoint of physical and mental stamina. With a short story you are never more than hours—or minutes—from the end of the chore.

A novel is an interminable effort. You think until you are weary. You write until you are ready to scream. You stop. You rest. But you have to get back to it. You have to pick up the threads, revive your enthusiasm, recapture the mood.

You have to do it day after day. Week after week.

When I was free-lancing in New York I wrote so much and for so long that there had to be an escape valve. I went to the movies. I went almost daily, sometimes twice in one day. I went to parties, to luncheons. I called on editors. Anything to get out of the house, to get away from the loneliness of writing.

I used to visit editors at least two days a week. There was no real reason to do it, once I was established. For several years I had a regular routine. On Mondays I always went into town (we lived in the suburbs after the first year). I made a call or two, then about eleven o'clock I would go to the offices of *Short Stories*. Bill Delaney and I talked awhile, or played a rubber or two of gin rummy, had lunch and returned and played some more gin rummy. About four or four-thirty I went home.

I always went into town on Fridays and frequently I found excuses to go in on another day or two.

During the seven years between 1934 and 1941 I wrote an average of six hundred thousand words a year. During the last three years of this period I was already writing books and the wordage of the twelve or so books produced during this period, added to the shorter stories, brought my average per year to above eight hundred thousand words.

This is an enormous amount of writing, any way you slice it. The manual labor involved in typing eight hundred thousand words a year is considerable. I flogged the typewriter day and night. I flogged it in the early hours of the morning, I beat at it, late at night. I worked Saturdays and Sundays.

While I was pretty well established as a writer by 1937, the Hollywood adage of being only as good as your last picture was true to a certain extent in writing for the magazines. You could not let down for very long. You could get by with an indifferent story now and then, and you might even get a poor one published on rare occasions, but your work had to hold up to a certain standard. The editors had to like your stories and the readers of their magazines had to like them.

I knew so many writers in those days. I saw them come, I saw them go. I knew the difficulties they had in trying to carve out a spot for themselves, I knew the troubles they had to remain in those niches. I knew the sweat, the toil and the heartache that went into the work of the other writers because I was doing it myself.

Each of us had his own way of working. I was never one for the regular hours. I couldn't sit down to a typewriter at eight in the morning and work straight through until one o'clock, or five o'clock, or any specified time. I might work at eight o'clock in the morning but I might just as well break off at nine o'clock and not work again until nine o'clock at night. Or midnight, or even later. I might even go two or three days without working at all. But I still had to work. I still had to turn out my sixty or seventy thousand words each and every month. I still had to work out many complete story ideas in a month. I still had to invent so many different scenes for the stories. I had to come up with "amazing climaxes." I had to have my hero "snatch victory from apparent defeat."

I felt the need of artificial aids to stimulate my thinking in those days. There was a book called *Plotto* which had been written in old age by a one-time very prolific dime novel writer. It was supposed to suggest thousands of plots to the current writers who used it. I bought one for twenty-five dollars and never got a single plot from it. Someone else had a thing called Plot Genie, which consisted of a pack of cards each with a few ideas on it. The idea was that you were to shuffle the cards and deal yourself a hand, which hand was supposed to be a plot, each unique, each different. For me Plot Genie did not work.

I used to analyze stories. What elements were required? Over a period of time I evolved a formula for mystery short stories. It consisted of eleven elements. With these eleven elements in a mystery plot I could not miss. I used to work out each element at a time, concentrating on one until I had licked it, then going on to the next. Most writers of mysteries inject the eleven elements into their stories anyway, but by putting them down one at a time I became conscious of them. Once I had worked out these eleven elements, the job of coming up with plots for mystery stories was greatly simplified.

I did not create this eleven-point mystery plot formula at one time. I evolved it over a period of about two years beginning back in 1934. I had perfected it by about the middle of 1936.

To this day I claim that this plot formula is foolproof. You can write a perfectly salable mystery story with perhaps only seven or eight of these elements, but get them all into a story and you cannot miss.

Here are the eleven elements:
 1. Colorful hero
 2. Theme
 3. Villain
 4. Background
 5. Murder method
 6. Motive
 7. Clue
 8. Trick
 9. Action
10. Climax
11. Emotion

Each of the eleven points needs amplification. In general the line to follow is summed up in the word "unusual." Every one of the eleven points had to be "unusual."

1. THE HERO. A hero must be colorful. He must have an occupation that is colorful or he must *be* a colorful person. In general, I have followed the theory that a regular policeman or detective is not colorful. Just think a moment about the greatest detective in all detective fiction—Sherlock Holmes—and you will quickly grasp what I mean by colorful.

2. THEME. This, to me, is the most important element of any mystery story plot. By theme I mean subject matter, what the story is about in addition to, over and above, the ACTUAL MURDER plot. To illustrate:

Death at the Main is about fighting cocks. I give a reasonably inside account of how gamecocks are raised, how they are fought, etc. This is knowledge not possessed by the average reader and believe me, I did not know it until I read up on the subject for the purpose of this story.

My book, *The Lock and the Key* was about locksmiths. A liberal education in making locks and keys was thrown into the murder plot. I knew absolutely nothing about locks and keys until I did research on the subject. I know no more than is in the book.

If you have ever read Dorothy Sayres' excellent English mysteries, you will find that theme figures superbly. In *The Nine Tailors* the reader learns all about church

bells, the art of bell-ringing, etc. In *Murder Must Adver-*
tise, Miss Sayres discusses advertising in all its phases.

However . . . knowledge of a subject should be used
sparingly. The mystery reader may not be as interested
in the subject as you are.

3. VILLAIN. Let's face it, the hero of detective
fiction is a superman. The villain must therefore be a
super-superman or have plenty of assistants. The odds
must ALWAYS be against the hero.

4. BACKGROUND. The story must be played
against a colorful or unusual background. The streets of
a big city are not necessarily colorful. If they're not,
make them so.

5. MURDER METHOD. Here again the "unu-
sual" should be considered. Shooting, stabbing, etc. are
acceptable, but the circumstances surrounding them
should be "unusual."

6. MOTIVE. Actually, there are only two reasons
for murder—hate and greed, but there are many subdi-
visions of these and the "motive" should be as unusual
as possible.

7. CLUE. Somewhere in the story there must be a
clue for the alert reader. Sure, try to fool the reader, but
the clue must be there if the reader should want to check
back on you after the story is over.

8. TRICK. In the grand finale, when all seems lost,
when the hero cannot possibly win out, he must snatch
victory from apparent defeat. By a trick . . . and here
again the word "unusual" applies.

181

9. ACTION. The story must have pace and move-
ment. It must not consist of talk, talk, talk about the
missing button, etc.

10. CLIMAX. A grand, smashing climax is necessary. Unusual.

11. EMOTION. The hero should be personally involved in some manner. He should be doing this over
and beyond the call of duty. Or beyond the money paid
him for doing it.

Chapter Twenty-five

In our bull sessions Heinie Faust once let drop a remark on which I pounced.

"I've written three hundred western books," he said, "and I've used only one plot."

"What was that plot?" I asked him.

"The good man becomes bad and the bad man becomes good. That way you have conflict. If the bad man stays bad and the good man stays good you have no conflict."

I thought of my own western stories. In most of them I had already done that very thing, although I had not been conscious of it. After this talk with Faust I remained conscious of it and it has been the theme of most of my westerns.

"The heavies" or villains in my stories have always appealed to me more than the good guys. I have written much of outlaws and gunfighters who are really "bad guys." They start bad and become good, whereas the "good guys," the respectable citizens in my stories usually become bad.

I never worked out a foolproof plot formula for westerns like the eleven-point plan for mysteries, but I did analyze them continuously in the hope that I could develop an aid to plotting them.

I came to the conclusion that there were only seven basic western stories. All westerns had to fit into one of these categories. Once I had these classifications worked out thoroughly it was of great help to me. I could go over them, decide that I had written stories in one or another of the groups only recently and it might be easier to do one of the others.

Deciding on one classification I could now concentrate on story ideas that would fit into this group.

Here are the seven basic western stories:

1. *The Union Pacific Story.* Into this classification fall all stories that have to do with the construction of a railroad, telegraph or stagecoach line. Stories of wagon trains crossing the plains and mountains, accounts of building toll roads, also fall into this grouping. Zane Grey's *The U.P. Trail* is a fine example of the Union Pacific Story. So is Ernest Haycox's *Trouble Shooter,* filmed as "Union Pacific."

2. *The Ranch Story.* This category includes stories laid on cattle ranches, stories of rustlers, of ranchers versus nesters, of cattlemen versus sheepmen—the typical cow-country story with typical cow-country horses and villains.

3. *The Empire Story.* This is not to be confused with Story No. 2, although it frequently has elements of "The Ranch Story" in it. In the "Empire Story" everything is on the grand scale.

If the story has a ranch it is of tremendous size, such as The King Ranch. The people, however, are more important than the problems of squatters, the fights over waterholes, fencing, rustlers.

The conflict is between titans of the West, man against man, man against history.

4. *The Revenge Story.* Someone has been wronged and the chief protagonist devotes months, years to a relentless pursuit of the wrong-doer, eventually bringing him to retribution. The most notable example of this type of story is Zane Grey's memorable *Riders of the Purple Sage,* considered by many the greatest western novel ever written.

5. *Custer's Last Stand.* This is simply the Cavalry and Indian story, although it may not have to do with Custer or the Little Big Horn. The cavalry and Indian story is basic and there is never a year without three or four good novels in this category. A change has come into this story, however, in recent years. In the old days the villains were the Indians. Today the villain is the white man. The Indian is persecuted, maligned, mistreated by the whites and massacres the whites only in retaliation.

6. *The Outlaw Story.* This is perennial fodder for the western fan. You can do Jesse James and Billy the Kid once every three or four years, and you can fill in with Sam Bass, Butch Cassidy or any fictitious outlaw. If your outlaw is your lead you must treat him with sympathy. He was forced into outlawry by people, conditions, The War.

7. *The Marshal Story.* This is the dedicated law-

man, so ably depicted in "High Noon," by Matt Dillon in "Gunsmoke" or by Jim Hardie in "Tales of Wells Fargo."

These seven basic western plots are quite enough. It is not the plot that is important, it is what you do with the characters, the incidental material, the conflicts, the emotions that are plumbed.

. . . and please don't bother to send me the eighth western plot. The seven basic western plots received considerable publicity some years ago and some hundreds of people mailed the "eighth" plot to me. There wasn't one of them that couldn't be fitted into one of the seven basic western plots.

Chapter Twenty-six

Nineteen hundred and sixty-seven.

Having practiced the art of creating suspense for so many years, I realize that I cannot leave unanswered the fate of some of the stories I have referred to in this recital.

Check back to the episode of Bill Dozier and *The French Key*. I had gone to him because he had sold a "first" mystery novel for ten thousand dollars. I had that figure in my mind and made a solemn vow to myself that I would one day get it for a mystery novel. I hoped that it would be for *The French Key*, but after years of waiting I began to doubt it.

I wrote *The French Key* early in 1939. I came to Hollywood in 1942. During those three years I never got an offer from a motion picture company for *The French Key* although the different agents I had from time to time all told me that they thought it was a good book and that they had some nibbles on it. But none of the nibbles became bites.

Yet I had hardly arrived in Hollywood than I received a bona fide offer for it. The amount offered was a trifle below the ten thousand dollar figure I had in my mind. In fact, it was for fifteen per cent of that—fifteen hundred dollars.

I came down from ten thousand dollars to twenty-five hundred dollars. The producer would not come up from his fifteen hundred dollar figure. Another producer came up with a smashing offer. Seven hundred fifty dollars. Yes, seven *hundred* and fifty dollars. I told the producer that I *had* seven hundred fifty dollars, I didn't need it. Soon, I had a third offer. This time it was for twenty-five hundred dollars, for which sum I had been willing to sell to the first producer.

I received three or four other offers during the next year or two, none for more than twenty-five hundred dollars. I turned them all down.

In 1945 I was finally vindicated. I sold *The French Key*—for fourteen thousand dollars.

My first novel, *Peace Marshal*, which had been rejected by the New York "top" agents as absolute trash, was made into a motion picture starring Richard Dix. Retitled "The Kansan," it has played on the late, late TV shows perhaps as often as any motion picture ever made.

It was reprinted in hard covers by Grosset & Dunlap, has been translated into eighteen languages. It was the first western book taken on by the Council of Books in Wartime and has been reprinted in seven different editions by paperback houses, with total sales of over one million copies.

While I am the first to concede that many of the

stories I wrote during the 1930's were trash, the fate of some of them is interesting. A *Black Mask* novelette, "The Sad Serbian" has been reprinted in seventeen anthologies of "best stories." It has sold to television three times (one time rights each sale).

Many, many other stories have been reprinted in anthologies. A fantasy, "The Thirteenth Floor," has gone into eighteen anthology printings and is currently in a Harper & Row High School English Reader.

Twenty-five or thirty of these old stories have sold to television.

My novels have done exceedingly well in paperback editions. They have done even better in foreign editions; some eight hundred fifty editions have been published in twenty-four different countries for total sales, as of this writing, in excess of ninety million copies.

In Hollywood I have written sixty-five feature motion picture screenplays. I created three successful TV series, "Tales of Wells Fargo," "The Texan," and "Shotgun Slade." I wrote possibly one hundred TV scripts.

Twenty-five of my books have sold to motion pictures. I have also sold a substantial number of "original" screenplays.